LOFTNESS

INCREASING PRODUCTIVITY AND PROFIT IN THE WORKPLACE

INCREASING PRODUCTIVITY AND PROFIT IN THE WORKPLACE

A Guide to Office Planning and Design

M. Glynn Shumake, AIA

JOHN WILEY & SONS, INC.

New York / Chichester / Brisbane / Toronto / Singapore

Copyright © 1992 by John Wiley & Sons, Inc.

This publication is designed to provide accurate and authoritative information in regard to the subject matter covered. It is sold with the understanding that the publisher is not engaged in rendering legal, accounting, or other professional services. If legal advice or other expert assistance is required, the services of a competent professional person should be sought. *From a Declaration of Principles jointly adopted by a Committee of the American Bar Association and a Committee of Publishers.*

Library of Congress Cataloging in Publication Data:

Shumake, M. Glynn.
    Increasing productivity and profit in the workplace : a guide to office planning and design / M. Glynn Shumake.
       p.   cm.
    Includes bibliographical references.
    ISBN 0-471-55893-1 (cloth)
    1. Office layout. 2. Industrial productivity. 3. Interior architecture. 4. Environmental engineering. 5. Office furniture.
    6. Facility management. I. Title.
HF5547.2.S58   1992   92-990
658.2′3—dc20   CIP

Printed in the United States of America

10 9 8 7 6 5 4 3 2 1

To Nancy whose inspiration and encouragement caused
this book to be written.

PREFACE

This book, as a reference, is intended to provide information for anyone who has a need to improve white collar productivity. As a tool the book may be used by anyone who must cause white collar productivity to actually happen. The book applies equally to any size of organization and it matters not whether the intent is to redo a portion of an existing workplace or the entire workplace. Similarly it is invaluable if your task is to create an entirely new facility in the same building, old or new, or in a different building, old or new.

I am not a journalist. I am an architect who for many years has specialized in interior architecture. Interior architecture, I would like to explain, includes everything in a building except the outside facing or skin of the outer walls, and the site, or land on which the building is located. As an interior architect I am particularly interested in what happens inside a building. Does the building, or a particular part of a building, provide the environment in which to efficiently perform the functions that are intended to be performed there? Too often the answer is no. Unless a structure is the Washington Monument or Saarinen's Arch, or something similar, the only justification for erecting it is to provide a place for the function that is to be carried out therein.

The methods and techniques presented in this book were discovered and perfected almost a decade ago. I waited to write this book, believing that since so many businessmen and their managers were seeking ways to reduce their operating costs and increase their profit, that a natural progression would cause the same discovery by others.

It seems, however, that small discoveries are easier to accept than large ones. The old adage *If it seems too good to be true, it probably is*, seems to make otherwise astute businessmen become extremely cautious and fearful, even after being presented with testimony by a client who has experienced a successful program.

I begin Part I with a general overview of the prevailing situation and attitude relative to improving productivity in the white collar workplace and continue with an introduction to different approaches to improving white collar productivity. Part II goes on to provide instruction and direction for achieving such improvement.

The solutions that I describe and recommend do not necessitate changing the way workers think or feel, or even the way they do their work; although such change may occur as the result of using the methods and techniques described in the book.

Numerous articles have been written on the subject of white collar productivity. Although some of the articles have touched on various parts of the approach or solutions that are presented in the book, none to my knowledge, has combined them as a complete solution to a major part of the white collar productivity problem.

The identification of specific deterrents to white collar productivity is original work by the author. So also is the development of new techniques, and the utilization of previously conceived methods, in combination, to reduce or remove those deterrents; and the identification and assignment of deterrents into the Alpha, Beta, Delta and Gamma divisions, or sectors.

I believe that the introduction and description of the Shumake Beta Module is in itself worth the cost of the book. This new concept workmodule is designed to support, and to be conducive to maximum productivity by an individual worker at any level of a business organization.

The material in the book has been successfully tested in the field through an active consulting relationship between the author and his clients or the clients of firms he has represented.

I believe that this book will be of great value to the thousands of business people and their managers who are required daily to seek solutions to the white collar productivity improvement problem. Also the book will be valuable to their facilities managers who must formulate plans to implement those solutions. Profit is a goal of virtually every legitimate business in existence; and reducing the cost of operation by improving white collar productivity is one way to achieve such a goal. This book explains how that may be accomplished.

The information in this book will also serve as a tool for architects, interior designers, and various other consultants who provide important advice to management and who are seeking new ways to improve the services they offer.

It is my intention that this book provide information and serve as a tool for businessmen, their business managers, and their facilities managers, in addition to architects, interior designers, and various other professionals. I have written it in a manner that I believe will make it easy to understand and simple to implement by all of the people who are in those capacities.

M. GLYNN SHUMAKE, AIA

St. Louis, Missouri
May 1992

CONTENTS

II THE PRODUCTIVE WORKPLACE: WHAT IT TAKES

I

THE CONCEPT

INTRODUCTION

The problems of white-collar productivity improvement may be approached from one of four directions. Each approach, or sector, has specific controls and limits that are determined by the deterrents attached to the sector. Each Control Sector is concerned with only one particular aspect of white-collar productivity.

CONTROL SECTORS OF THE WORKPLACE

The Alpha Sector

The Alpha Sector deals with the individual as a person: the way that particular person thinks, the way that particular person feels, and who and what they are.

The Beta Sector

The Beta Sector is involved with the physical aspects of the workplace: the workstations and the workmodules, the furniture systems and the building systems, and the various materials used for construction and finishes.

The Gamma Sector

The Gamma Sector has to do with equipment: mechanical, electrical, or electronic machines that extend the physical and mental abilities of the individual.

The Delta Sector

The Delta Sector is concerned with procedures, techniques, and methods for performing the tasks of the workplace. In addition, this sector is responsible for the quality of work materials.

Each of these sectors impacts greatly on the amount of work any individual produces. And each of these sectors has limiters in the form of deterrents, which

3

ultimately control the amount of productivity that can be expected from each individual under any set of circumstances and conditions (see Chapter 2).

Beta Control Sector

Although each Control Sector is very important, since each contributes a major portion of the total productivity output of an organization, the Beta Control Sector is the area of white-collar productivity improvement that is addressed in this book.

The solutions that follow later are not a panacea. They will not solve all of the problems of the world. They will not even solve all of the problems of the white-collar workplace. What these solutions will do is provide the means to bring about substantial improvement in white-collar productivity for any business, regardless of size.

As with virtually any project or tool that is designed to be cost effective there is a premium to pay. It is still necessary to "pay to play." Although these solutions have a high return-on-investment potential, a short payback period, and are simple to accomplish when properly installed and implemented, there is a premium as well.

That is the bad news. The good news is that you can get all of your investment, all of your premium back, then go on to add handsomely to your bottom line. When the payback is completed the benefits continue to accumulate, through reduced operating cost, as increased profit potential.

Remember, if your workplaces are not paying their own way, something is very wrong. Because *They Should Be*!

Another fact to be considered by any group or individual attempting to increase white-collar productivity is that the person or persons attempting such change must have either substantial management control or management cooperation if their project is to be a success. When you create the potential for increased productivity, management cooperation is necessary to ensure that the maximum improvement in white-collar work output will occur and that the success of the project will not be limited to what occurs just because it is easier for the workers to do their jobs. In addition, these or any other white-collar productivity improvement techniques or methods cannot overcome bad management.

This book deals only with the Beta deterrents or the external aspects of white-collar productivity improvement. External, in this sense, simply means there is no attempt to motivate or to make behavioral changes directly.

The term gold-collar workers refers to workers who because of their knowledge command higher salaries. The cost difference between white-collar and gold-collar workers is an important factor for management to keep in mind. Gold-collar workers cost you more per worker than white-collar workers. From the standpoint of productivity improvement in the Beta Sector this is the principal difference.

If you are going to do a pilot study, it is prudent to consider doing the study with gold-collar workers. The payback is quicker and the gains are potentially higher. Virtually all of the other factors are essentially the same.

For some time now the idea of making major gains in the improvement of the white-collar output has been viewed by many, if not most, as a formidable task with little, if any, chance for success. It is a task that is often faced with fear and wonderment and with an approach somewhat like the thinking that existed for years about breaking the sound barrier—it is something to continually try for, but most likely something that cannot be achieved.

On the surface the problems involved with solving the white-collar productivity dilemma may seem overwhelming; however, there are only two deterrent problems to be solved, and although each of these problems contains a number of facets, the techniques and methods for the resolution of each are available, as presented in the pages that follow.

1

WHITE-COLLAR PRODUCTIVITY IMPROVEMENT

In view of the negative writing and reports that have been produced in recent years telling how the workers of America have little, if any, desire to work and are unwilling to take on responsibilities, why even bother to try to improve productivity?

WHY BOTHER?

If, indeed, the workers who make up this white-collar work force do not want to work or do a good job, then the idea of improving their output is preposterous and not worth the time it takes to discuss it.

If, on the other hand, the workers are willing to work, are not lazy, and are interested in producing work they can be proud of, then it is worth not only discussion, but also consideration and support from management at all levels. Ultimately, when productivity increases in any sector, everyone can and should be pleased and should also share in the benefits.

Writing in *Psychology Today*, Daniel Yankelovich refers to a 1980 Gallup Study for the United States Chamber of Commerce that, he says,

> shows that an overwhelming 88 percent of all working Americans feel that it is personally important to them to work hard and do their best on the job. . . . The study concludes that a faulty work ethic is not responsible for the decline in our productivity; quite the contrary, the study identifies "a widespread commitment among U.S. workers to improve productivity" and suggests that "there are large reservoirs of potential upon which management can draw to improve performance and increase productivity."*

*Reprinted with permission from *Psychology Today* magazine, copyright © 1982, Sussex Publishers, Inc.

Too often the argument has been made that the important area to be concerned with, in any manufacturing operation, is the plant itself, where the product is actually being produced. Somehow if you can just get the productivity problem resolved there, the rest of the operation will move along quite satisfactorily. If this is true, why be concerned with trying to improve white-collar productivity?

One reason for seeking such improvement is that for some time white-collar productivity has accounted for most of the work output in the United States. This fact alone means that for any business that employs white-collar workers, whatever the number, there is a vested interest in increasing the productivity of that group as a means of decreasing the cost of operating the business.

In many businesses white-collar workers make up the entire work force. When this is the case there is all the more reason to reduce the largest single cost of virtually any organization, labor, in the interest of increasing the primary goal of every organization, profit. As you will read further on, the information society, white collar America, is upon us and is increasing at a phenomenal rate.

INFORMATION PROCESSORS

According to John Naisbitt in his book *Megatrends* (1982), the information society began in 1956 when,

> for the first time in American history, white-collar workers in technical, managerial and clerical positions outnumbered blue-collar workers. Industrial America was giving way to a new society, where, for the first time in history, most of us worked with information rather than producing goods.*

He continues,

> The following year—1957—marked the beginning of the globalization of the information revolution. The Russians launched Sputnik, the missing technological catalyst in a growing information society. The real importance of Sputnik is *not* that it began the space age, but that it introduced the era of global satellite communications.*

Further on Mr. Naisbitt, referring to the end of the industrial era and the resulting changes in the workforce, says,

> The real increase has been in information occupations. In 1950, only about 17 percent of us worked in information jobs. Now, more than 60 percent of us work with information as programmers, teachers, clerks, secretaries, accountants, stock brokers, managers, insurance people, bureaucrats, lawyers, bankers and

*Reprinted with permission of Warner Books, New York, from *Megatrends*, copyright © 1982 by John Naisbitt.

technicians. And many more workers hold information jobs within manufacturing companies. Most Americans spend their time creating, processing, or distributing information.*

Mr. Naisbitt also reports that

> Professional workers are almost all information workers—lawyers, teachers, engineers, computer programmers, system analysts, doctors, architects, accountants, librarians, newspaper reporters, social workers, nurses and clergy. Of course everyone needs some kind of knowledge to do a job. Industrial workers, machinists, welders, jig makers, for example, are very knowledgeable about the tasks they perform. The difference is that for professional and clerical workers, the creation, processing and distribution of information *is* the job.*

The need to improve white collar productivity has become more urgent as a result of the change in the ratio of information workers to laborers. The opportunity for such improvement has been available to us all along. Based on conventional thinking of the past, however, it was not important enough to be concerned with. Now, because of the vast number of people who are part of this group, it can no longer be ignored.

All of us who work in the white-collar sector are information processors. There are those who actually create new information and there are those whose primary function is to distribute information after it has been processed. But all of us are processors of various amounts of information as part of, if not all, the work we do each day as we pursue our particular career or profession.

If all of the people who deal in any way with information are thought of as information processors, it may help to understand why methods and techniques that are described here are able to bring about dramatic improvement in performance.

WHITE-COLLAR PRODUCTIVITY

Productivity in general and white collar productivity in particular have more than one definition. Each definition has various points to be made based on particular assumptions. For the purposes of this book it is not necessary to argue for or against any of these. Rather we will present definitions as they apply to the problem, as well as the solution presented herein.

The majority of businesses are quite satisfied to receive an efficient individual work performance from their white-collar workers. "Efficient," according to Webster's *New Collegiate Dictionary*, means

> productive of desired effects; *esp*: productive without waste.†

*Reprinted by permission of Warner Books, New York, from *Megatrends*, copyright © 1982 by John Naisbitt.

†By permission. From Webster's *Ninth New Collegiate Dictionary* © 1991 by Merriam-Webster Inc., publisher of the Merriam-Webster® dictionaries.

What we are seeking, then, is to have all of our information workers deliver the desired results of their particular job description, preferably without waste, that is, error free, or at the very least with the highest degree of accuracy possible.

Overall, the desired effect is to have the most work done by the least number of people in the least amount of time. At the individual level the goal is exactly the same. The specifics of each task and job description may vary, but the goal of virtually every businessman is to have those tasks performed, accurately, in the least amount of time. Such a goal, when successfully attained, translates into receiving the most work for the least cost, thereby creating the potential for the most profit. And, after all, for most people that is what business is all about.

2

THE DETERRENTS

I stated in the introduction that anyone attempting to deal with the problems of white-collar productivity improvement must approach the problem from one of four directions because the production flowing from workers is controlled and limited by essentially four sets of deterrents (see Table 2.1).

ALPHA SECTOR DETERRENTS

The deterrents of the Alpha Sector are dictated by the personality of each individual worker: the way that person thinks, the way that person feels about everything, his or her priorities, and prejudices. It includes a multitude of things that contribute to the uniqueness of that person.

In addition to the internal forces in each of us, there are external influences that affect the way we behave as individuals. These external influences include, but are not limited to, family members, friends, and peers. In addition, there are religious and political beliefs, and, in some instances, even varying degrees of mental illness will be found as a deterrent of this set. Improving productivity through change in the alpha Sector requires adjustments in individual attitudes, opinions, and behavior, and the correction of any detrimental habits.

Usual methods for change in the Alpha Sector include incentives and other motivators that are used as a means to bring about voluntary change by each worker. Motivators or incentives that bring about change in some workers, however, may have absolutely no effect on others. This type of change may be difficult to accomplish and slow to be realized. In addition, it is somewhat unpredictable and results may be short term, requiring new motivators or new incentives for continued productivity gains; or in some instances just to maintain previous levels of achievement.

The techniques and methods described in this book, when properly applied, may actually result in changes in the attitude and behavior of some employees. When this does occur, it is certainly welcome. It should be noted, however, that such changes are coincidental and are not the primary goals of the guidelines and instructions in this book.

BETA SECTOR DETERRENTS

Beta Sector Deterrents are those that occur as a result of physical surroundings—the interior environment. This includes furniture and systems furniture, equipment, and materials that the individual uses, comes into contact with, or is proximate to, while performing his or her work. Unlike the Alpha deterrents, the Beta deterrents are controllable in a predictable manner.

Methods of change in the Beta Sector involve the appropriate use of specific furniture, equipment, and materials, each of which contributes to optimizing the workplace by reducing, neutralizing, or eliminating the Beta deterrents.

GAMMA SECTOR DETERRENTS

Gamma Sector deterrents are caused in some instances by the presence and in other instances by the absence of certain devices. The Gamma Sector involves making individuals more capable than they otherwise would be. This is accomplished by extending individual physical and mental abilities by augmenting them with machines, or other tools that are used to improve the quality or increase the quantity of the white-collar work produced.

Methods of change in the Gamma Sector require adding necessary devices to improve productivity. In other situations it may be necessary to take away inappropriate equipment to cause the desired improvement in production.

Gamma deterrents, those physical and mental limitations we have because we are human, can be reduced, or in some instances eliminated, by the use of electronic and mechanical devices such as telephones, typewriters, and computers.

DELTA SECTOR DETERRENTS

Delta Sector deterrents are the result of inappropriate, incorrect, cumbersome, outdated, or even unnecessary procedures and methods. Additional deterrents of the Delta Sector are caused by poor quality work materials.

Changes in the Delta Sector occur as the result of reviewing existing procedures and then adding procedures that are needed, modifying procedures that are flawed, for whatever reason, and removing procedures that are found to be inappropriate, outdated or unnecessary. Further changes are accomplished by reviewing all work materials, printed information, and forms of all kinds relative to print quality, contrast, and logic and clarity of instructions and data.

THE BETA DETERRENTS

Seeking ways to improve white collar productivity can at first appear to be very difficult and complicated. A number of years ago, while searching for solutions to what I perceived to be the many problems of white-collar productivity, I discovered that the path always seemed to lead back to the same small number of points. Later, while trying to define individual segments of the main problem, the same sequence kept recurring. At first the segment would lead to just a few sources; but the same sources. Eventually with each and every segment the path would lead to one of just two points; or obstacles to white-collar productivity improvement.

It became obvious that solving productivity problems in the Beta Sector relied entirely on our ability to minimize, neutralize, or remove completely just two deterrents. Although each of these deterrents has a number of facets, there are only two deterrent categories to be dealt with:

1. Sensory Distraction
2. Fatigue

To whatever extent these two deterrents are reduced, to a similar extent white-collar productivity potential will be increased. To improve white-collar productivity in the Beta Sector one must remove or reduce these deterrents to the greatest extent possible. As the productivity potential rises, so does profit potential.

Sensory Distraction

Distraction through the five senses accounts for the major portion of inadvertent disruption of and interference with white-collar productivity. Of these, disruption through the sense of sight is most likely to cause distraction, but is rather easy to control.

An example is the situation where a co-worker has been on maternity leave and this is the day she returns to introduce the new baby. The new mother enters an area with 50 desks in a large open area. The result is the same if there are only five desks. Even if the new mother intends to speak to only a few of the workers in the area, almost all of the workers will be distracted for varying amounts of time depending on specific interest and the actions of mother, baby, and co-workers.

This situation can be controlled by restricting the area of view available to each worker. The amount of distraction is then limited in relation to the area of view available.

Disturbance through the sense of hearing is equally distracting but much more difficult to control since the offending sound may originate a considerable distance from the point where the distraction or distractions are occurring.

An example is a situation in which workers pass through or near your area to get the snack bar or lunchroom. Although the workers who are passing through cannot be seen by your workers, their conversations can be easily heard. During various periods of the day distractions occur and do affect the productivity of your people.

This situation can be remedied by different methods. One is to reconfigure the entire area to create new passage routes. If that is not feasible there are methods and materials that can be used to absorb the sound, reducing it to a level at which it no longer distracts.

As shown by these examples, a single sensory distraction may affect many individuals, disrupting their work situation and adversly affecting their productivity. Distraction through the remaining senses of smell, taste, and feel, although less frequent, are worthy of attention inasmuch as such interference is also a detriment to your organization's productivity.

Fatigue

Fatigue is inherent in all of the things we do, the things we see, the tools we use, and the many things with which we come in contact. Fatigue is built into the workstations we use, the various types of lighting used to illuminate our workspaces and all of the other elements of the workplace.

Each of us, when we awake, is at our peak for the day in energy and mental capacity, unless we are ill or incapacitated in some other way. From that point on we begin to spend each of these assets and we continue to spend them throughout our work day until, exhausted, we return to rest at the end of the day. This can best be shown by the curve in Figure 2.1.

We begin the day at a high position on the chart. Most of us continue on a fairly flat plane until late morning when our curve begins to turn downward, through the lunch hour and into early afternoon, at which time the curve begins a precipitous plunge until it is time to leave the workplace for the day.

Everything we do, as we proceed through our day, has an energy and mental resource price tag. These expenditures are the result of fatigue factors. If white-collar productivity is to improved, it is necessary to improve all fatigue factors associated with workmodules furniture, equipment, and all other physical elements of the workplace, as much as possible.

When we are successful in reducing fatigue factors sufficiently, the flat portion of the white-collar workers' curve extends farther into the day and the

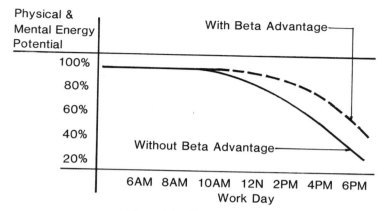

Figure 2.1. Efficiency curve.

curve is higher at the end of the day. The significance of this fact is this. If the curve is higher at the end of the day, the workers feel better when they leave for the day. More important, however, is the fact that the workers feel better about returning to the workplace the following morning.

As an example of what constitutes a fatigue factor that can be minimized or eliminated, consider the top of your desk or worksurface. What color is it? More important, is it dark or light? Let us assume that you have a dark-colored worksurface. It may be walnut wood, plastic laminate, or it may be brown linoleum. Now consider the papers and other items you work with on your desk each day. Most of these are white or light colored.

Your eyes scan the worksurface as you go about your job, and the irises of your eyes open and close, controlling the amount of light that enters. As your eyes pass from the dark worksurface to the light work material the irises close down; then as the eyes continue on from light to dark again the irises open to allow more light to enter.

This process, which is involuntary, continues throughout the entire day and is tiring to your eyes and your brain. This is only one of many fatigue factors that must be eliminated if your workers are ever to achieve the productivity level of which they are capable and of which the majority of workers would like to deliver.

In this situation the solution is to reduce the contrast between the worksurface top material and the work materials used thereon. A light gray, gray/green (putty), or beige color for the worksurface is better than any dark color. Although white is light, it often is actually too light, or bright. A white worksurface can cause a different kind of fatigue factor, glare. Any glossy finish for worksurfaces should be avoided because it will act as a mirror and reflect light from ceiling fixtures into the workers eyes; this is still another fatigue factor.

Reaching for work materials, such as files, reference folders, pencils, or paper clips, reaching to replace work materials and items, and reaching to operate some piece of equipment are all actions that require energy, and each involves fatigue factors. A completely efficient workstation will allow you to do the majority of your work tasks without substantially changing your position, except to rotate your chair. The closer to that ideal your workstation and workmodule are, the fewer fatigue factors there will be to deplete your physical and mental energy supply. Worksurfaces greater than 24 inches in depth require an excess expenditure of physical energy and an excess amount of time while reaching. Most of us cannot reach further than 24 inches without moving out of our work-intensive position. Materials that are accessed or used more than once a day should be kept above the top of the worksurface in open shelves. If shelves must be locked for security reasons at night, then the doors for shelves should be such that they can be stored in the open position during the time when the individual is working in the workstation.

Worksurfaces and the shelves above them should be positioned at a height to accommodate the size of the individual worker. If the person is short the worksurface and shelf above it should be lowered to the proper height above the floor. If the person is tall then the components need to be adjusted to a higher level. The relationship between the top of the worksurface and surface of the shelf on which books or binders are placed should also be adjusted in accordance with the individual.

Table 2.1. White-Collar Productivity Limit/Control Sectors

Limit Control Elements	Alpha (People)	Beta (Interior Environment)	Gamma (Tools)	Delta (Methods and Procedures)

	Motivation
	Incentives
	Change
	  The way people think
	  The way people behave
	People's attitudes
	People's bad habits
		Workstation design
		Workstation configuration
		Individual workstation
		Relative workstation
		Materials of the workplace
		Horizontal surfaces
		Vertical surfaces
		Lighting (ambient and task)
		Window treatment
		Electronic sound masking
			Extension of human physical abilities
			  Mechanical
			  Electrical
			  Electronic
				Improve paper flow and communication procedures
				  Review
				  Modify
				  Eliminate
				  Add
				  Software

Goal	Improve the people	Improve the interior environment	Improve the inherent ability of the people	Improve the organization and process of the work
Current Effort	Largest effort	Rehash of old ideas and techniques	Much incidental effort	Varied effort
Results	Big business/most difficult to accomplish and sustain	Accidental results; least difficult to accomplish and sustain	Varying results as new products become available	Business as usual; varying results

17

3

PROBLEMS OF THE WORKPLACE ENVIRONMENT

In the preceding chapter we explained how the two deterrents, sensory distraction and fatigue, reduce productivity for virtually all workers. The problem then is that there are a sufficient number of these deterrents in most workplaces to seriously reduce the productivity of white-collar workers who work there. The problem is also how to remove as many factors as possible that contribute to and/or support either of these deterrents. Sounds simple, and to a large degree it is. Knowing what to look for, and what to do about it when you find it, is what this book is about.

SOURCES OF SENSORY DISTRACTION

Most of us take the five types of sensors attached to our bodies pretty much for granted, even forgotten, until something goes wrong with one of them or until one of the sensors detects something that detracts us from whatever it is we are doing. The distraction may offend us or it may please us. At any rate it gets our attention.

The sensors are, of course, our eyes, our ears, our nose, our taste buds, and the nerve endings that allow us to measure variously through the sense of touch.

Sensory distraction in the workplace is mostly the result of sights and sounds that are normally encountered there. Sights in the workplace require only two conditions to become sight distractions. First, an individual must be able to see what is happening. Second, the act or occurrence seen must be of sufficient interest to penetrate the worker's consciousness. For workers who are concentrating deeply on the work tasks that they are performing, penetration will be more difficult, sometimes requiring a personal interest before a distraction occurs. For workers who are disinterested or bored with what they are doing, distraction is almost assured and quickly forthcomming.

AURAL DISTRACTIONS IN THE WORKPLACE

Sounds of the workplace are many. The more common sounds include those of typewriters, copiers, computer printers, telephones, and human voices. The voices, most often, are those of other workers who have workstations in the same area, or who may just be passing through the area.

Sounds that distract may originate outside of the area in which the distraction occurs and may even come from outside of the building. Sounds from the outside often include that of the siren on an emergency vehicle or the roar of a jet aircraft's engines as it passes overhead.

Sounds will enter the workstation from all directions. Sound will be transmitted through interior partitions; and it does not matter if the partitions are low, of medium height, or extend to the ceiling. Sound will penetrate through outside walls and windows and will enter the workspace having passed through the floor and ceiling above you as well as through the floor below you. Sound penetrates. Sound travels through the materials normally used in construction. In addition to sounds that enter the workspace from another area there are those sounds that originate in another part of the same area.

Impact sounds, for instance, are those that are caused by an object striking some portion of the building structure. Most frequently this type of sound, as heard in the workspace, is caused by shoe heels impacting on a hard floor surface, such as wood, marble, or terrazzo, or a relatively hard floor finish like vinyl tile or vinyl sheet goods. Such sounds can also be produced when a co-worker drops an object or pounds on a drawer that will not open properly.

Qualities that retard the passage of sound waves are mass and weight. Therefore if you are located in a totally concrete building or better still a lead-lined room, each with no doors or windows, less sound will penetrate. If each of the materials is sufficiently thick perhaps no sound will enter. However, such conditions are not usually encountered in the white-collar workplace, fortunately.

A sound may originate at some remote point in the building and then actually be transmitted through the structure, or its cavities and chases, traveling throughout a large portion of the building. Such sounds are transmitted through floors, partitions, and ceilings and into the workspaces. It is here that we not only hear them, but it is here that they become potential distractions, depending on how loud the sounds are. Except at time of construction, it is frequently difficult or impossible to reduce building-borne sounds, as such. Once such sounds are transmitted into the actual workplace as airborne sounds, however, they can be dealt with effectively.

HORIZONTAL SURFACES

The horizontal surfaces of a building consist primarily of the floors and ceilings. As we have just indicated and depending on the construction of each, varying amounts of distracting sound will penetrate the floor or ceiling and enter the workspace and the individual workstation. Sound may enter the ceiling plenum on one side of the partition enclosing a private office, pass over the top of that partition, be reflected off the structure of the floor or roof above and down through the ceiling into the private office. In such a situation, which is common in work places everywhere, there is no such thing as a confidential conversation to be held in that private office, no matter how well the partition itself stops the direct passage of sound.

VERTICAL SURFACES

Vertical surfaces of a building are the walls and partitions. These may be interior or exterior, short, or to the ceiling, or to the floor or roof structure above, and may be thick or thin and constructed in many different ways. The vertical surfaces of the workspace are valuable in helping to control visual distractions in the workspace. With very few exceptions all walls and partitions will allow the passage of distracting sound to some extent. Again, depending on the materials and the construction of each, a particular wall or partition may contribute greatly, or very little, toward absorbing or retarding the passage of sound. The surface of the vertical divider can be used to control the absorption or retardation of sound by altering the finish of the material.

VISUAL DISTRACTIONS IN THE WORKPLACE

Of all the distractions to white-collar workers in the workplace, the sensory distractions are probably the least recognized and the least understood. Distraction through the sense of sight, by occurrences that are seen and that originate within the workspace, may be caused by persons who are just passing through the area. It may be caused by individuals, such as construction or maintenance workers who are working in the same area or an adjacent one. It may also be caused by the employee on maternity leave who has just returned to show off the new baby.

Sensory distractions are those that we become aware of through information that is received by one of the various sensory devices of our body. These sensors are exposed to stimulation every day and react according to the way in which they have been programmed, trained, and conditioned throughout our lifetimes. Although all sensory distraction will cause a loss of productivity, those to which we succumb most frequently are the sense of sight and the sense of hearing. Although vertical surfaces in the workplace contribute to reducing distraction through both of these senses, we are addressing in this section the inadvertent distraction in the workplace through the sense of sight.

Sensory distractions will be seen by most individuals as distracting only if the experience is unpleasant. If the occurrence, even though distracting, is enjoyable, it is likely to be perceived as a distraction only by supervisors and managers. If the event is pleasant enough to the supervisors and managers, they too are unlikely to consider the situation as distracting. The only way to be reasonably certain that the happening will not be a distraction is to take steps to prevent its observance by anyone, or if that is not possible, to have the event seen by as few workers as possible.

Visualize a group of workers surrounded by panels about 4 feet (121.9 centimeters) along a passageway or corridor through which other individuals pass throughout the workday. Now focus a television camera on the eyes of each of these individuals, and let the cameras run as people continue their work. Viewing the monitors or video tape of what is seen by the camera, you will notice that as co-workers in the passageway pass those workers within the panel-enclosed area, a reaction will occur in the eyes of the enclosed workers. When the workers are concentrating heavily on the work that they are doing, not looking up, but actually looking at the work, a reaction will begin to occur as their visual sensors, their eyes, become aware that something is entering their range of observation, which is synonymous with the range of their peripheral vision. When individuals are concentrating heavily on their task, even though their head position does not change, their eyes will move without conscious command to determine the *risk* involved as a result of the intrusion. If workers are so deeply involved in their work that they never move their head, the eyes in some cases will attempt to follow the passing person until they are out of the visual range of the worker.

The worker is not thinking *Someone is coming*, or *Who is that*? The eyes, because of instinct, which conceivably goes back to the days when men and women lived in caves, are constantly on the alert, trying to determine if an attack is about to occur, or if they were about to be injured or killed. If that takes you too far back then consider that since the day we were born we have been cautioned to be careful to watch out, to look around us, to know what the situation is, and, whether we consciously do those things or not, our brain subconsciously tries to do what it has been conditioned to believe is right; to do what is in our own best interest as far as safeguarding our being is concerned. So as our eyes make this detection, a signal is sent to the brain in an attempt to make our brain aware of, or to check into what is going on. Is it something to worry about or not? In any case we are being distracted.

Subconsciously there is a conflict taking place in our brain between ourselves, trying to concentrate to do whatever work process we are going through, and our visual sensors saying, Alert! Alert! Alert! Check it out! See what the problem is. See if there *is* a problem. Do something about it if necessary.

Now these may be ancient, or not so ancient, urgings, but they are very real. We can insist that such is not the case, but that does not change anything. It is similar to a person driving down the highway at sixty miles per hour when a tire blows out, and the driver says "No problem! We'll just go right ahead," and attempts to drive on down the highway. Financially, on an annual basis, the economic result of this type of distraction, repeated countless times every day in your workplace, can be similarly catastrophic.

The types of worker that we have been talking about are persons who have been concentrating on their work and are having a mental conflict as to whether to break their concentration to check out the detected intrusion into their visual zone. What about the other types of workers who are not concentrating. The person may be working, only slightly engrossed, they may be in neutral, or they may be doing absolutely nothing. When the distraction that we described above occurs, this type of worker may react in a number of different ways. If the individual who is passing by is unknown to the worker in the station, each may smile and then proceed with whatever they were doing previous to the encounter. If the passing co-worker is recognized by the worker in the station, instead of a smile perhaps greetings will be exchanged, or even a prolonged conversation before again continuing with their work. Each of these occurrences is a distraction and each of these does reduce your productivity.

In many distraction events of the type I have just described, the distraction is inadvertent. The person who does the distracting did not come there for that purpose. It is distraction of opportunity, but the result is the same; lost productivity. Inadvertent distraction is something that can be resolved, minimized, and in some instances eliminated altogether. Where distraction is intentional it is something altogether different and if someone is determined to distract another individual, there may be nothing that can be done to prevent it. Certainly the methods and techniques of the Beta Sector of productivity improvement will do very little to help. Intentional distraction of one individual by another is a totally different kind of management problem that must be met and solved in an entirely different manner.

We have talked about the problem of inadvertent distraction by co-workers, How do you solve it? The solution to this and other workplace problems is addressed in Chapter 4.

TRANSPARENT VERTICAL SURFACES

External sight distractions are usually limited to observations that occur as the result of looking through a window in an exterior wall to a view of the outside world or seeing through a glass partition or the borrow light glass of an interior wall that opens into an atrium, passage, or other area. This type of window or partiton material is a transparent vertical surface and if not properly treated or eliminated, presents potential productivity deterrent.

When the prospect of having workers in workmodules that are enclosed or partially enclosed by panels is presented, someone will frequently complain that their employees do not like to be in *cubicles* or *pods*. Often a solution is suggested shortly thereafter, and may be offered by virtually anyone involved in the design and planning process, the architect, the designer, a supervisor, a manager, the owner of the business, or individual workers themselves, and goes something like this. "If the workmodule can just have a small glass panel that the worker can see through, they won't feel so confined."

When it comes to the reduction of, or the prevention of, sensory distraction through the sense of sight as applies to glass partitions or glass panels in partitions, if you can see through it, it might as well not be there, referring to the glazed panel.

I have heard all sorts of arguments for placing glass in the walls of various areas. Conference rooms, for instance, with a wall of glass separating the conference area from the corridor that is located along one side of the conference area. Perhaps the single, most frequently given reason for having such a glass wall is that it lets outside light into the interior of the building. In some instances where that argument has been made, there were no windows in any of the three other walls of the conference area through which outside light could be obtained that could then be let into the interior of the building. More often the situation is that although there are a number of windows in the area with the interior glass wall, those windows are covered by draperies, vertical or horizontal blinds, or other solar and light-control devices that are tightly closed, most of the time.

As a designer's element, it is simply a way to showcase that area, a way to let people who may never get into those conference areas see how *beautiful* the rooms are. On many projects, a desire to open the areas for display is the only reason that there are glass walls in conference areas, offices, and individual workmodules. Although there are many varied explanations and arguments regarding the necessity of having glass walls in these areas, function cannot ordinarily be one of them.

The purpose of a meeting room or conference area is to provide a place where two or more people can meet to communicate with each other without distraction or interruption. The first thing that you need is the room itself, which can be as simple or as ornate as your taste and budget will allow. Add to that appropriate and comfortable furniture, whatever presentation, display, and storage units that are needed and you are ready to have your first conference. If you have a room with four solid walls, or three solid walls and windows to the outside and have vertical blinds, or other window treatments that are closed, your meeting can proceed, you have control, and communication takes place, without distraction and without interruption.

If one of the walls in the room is glass, and if that wall has no visual control device, then whoever is trying to conduct the meeting may have difficulty maintaining the attention of the participants. As a direct result of the distraction it may also be difficult to control the proceedings in a way that you would prefer.

I know of a corporation that has many of its own conference areas and offices lined with glass walls—at least one glass wall per room. I have held a number of meetings in those rooms and I know the problems that are caused by the glass walls and how they interfere with the function of the space. The distraction results, primarily, when individuals inside the room see others outside the room. There are many scenarios, but the results are the same, although the extent of the distraction and/or disruption will differ from incident to incident. The distraction may be due to mere curiosity. It may be flirtation. It may result from the desire of an individual inside the room to signal or otherwise communicate with someone outside the room, or vice versa. Whatever the cause, distraction occurs. The distraction may be limited to the individual involved. It may be noticed by one or more of the other participants, in which instance they too are distracted. In many cases the leader or presenter notices the action and becomes distracted. Depending on the leader's reaction, the entire meeting may be disrupted.

All of the problems associated with having glass walls or panels in conference areas apply equally to offices and to workmodules. Although each of these other types of areas may have only one occupant to be distracted, that individual's productivity may be reduced considerably by this type of distraction.

BRIGHTNESS AND GLARE

Our ability to see depends on brightness. Excessive brightness or glare interferes with our ability to see well, and under some conditions our ability to function normally for various periods of time. There are essentially two areas of the workplace that often have fatigue factor deterrents built in. These areas are the ceiling light fixtures and grid, and exterior windows.

Ceiling Brightness

At any time workers look at the ceiling they need to see a consistent and non-bright surface. The light fixtures are only slightly brighter than the surrounding ceiling, because of their parabolic louvers, and the ceiling grid is finished with flat or low-gloss paint.

When a worker looks up at the ceiling and sees brightness, whether it is caused by strong light reflecting off of the ceiling board or grid, or if it is caused by brightness on the surface of a flat-lensed light fixture, an after-image in the shape of the bright area or areas is formed in the eye of the worker. When workers return their eyes again to the material on which they are working, the after-image will appear to be suspended between the worker and the work material, or superimposed on the work material, obscuring the worker's view of that material. In a few moments the after-image will fade away and viewing by the worker will return to normal. During this period, however, that individual's productivity will be lessened. Over the course of an entire work day this action will occur a number of times. Measured on an annual basis this distraction will amount to a substantial number.

Window Brightness

The same kind of problem exists with any type of excessive brightness or glare. Windows without a means to control the brightness, or glare can be as distracting as light fixtures, or even more, since the levels of these conditions are potentially higher. Depending on the location of your building and its orientation, the sun's rays will penetrate directly into workspaces, particularly on the east side of the structure in the early morning and the west side in the late afternoon. Heat from the sun can be uncomfortable, and its brightness can be unbearable. The appropriate shading device will allow these problems to be controlled from a comfort viewpoint.

If these devices are chosen for energy conservation purposes, they may be automatically controlled and operated by sensors that identify the need and close the devices. Some of the most severe problems with window brightness and glare will not occur on a sunny day, however. On certain days when there is an overcast sky that the sun illuminates with its diffuse radiation, the brightness levels will be very high at the windows. Any worker who looks at an unshielded window surface may very well be temporarily blinded by the brightness, and retain an after-image for some moments.

Other Brightness

If the workstation shelves or cabinets from which task lights are suspended are mounted high enough, light from the fixture may shine into the worker's eyes causing the same type of problems and distraction as ceiling fixtures.

Worksurfaces, if they are too reflective (white) or too shiny (highly polished finish), can cause a fatigue factor deterrent. And it matters not whether the worksurface is suspended from a systems furniture panel or is the top of an executive's desk. Such surfaces can reflect images of ceiling fixtures and their light sources directly into the eyes of the workers. Such reflections can be distracting and can cause headaches and eye irritation over long periods.

4

THE WORKPLACE SOLUTION

There is no simple solution to the interior problem. Rather, the solution for the interior is composed of a number of facets, each of which contributes part of the answer to the problem of productivity lost due to distraction and fatigue. A number of the solution segments deal with acoustical treatment, others provide sight barriers, while still others reduce fatigue factors.

SIGHT BARRIERS

An old saying, "Out of sight, out of mind," is appropriate in explaining one of the most prevalent sensory distractions.

If you cannot see something that happens, you do not know that it is happening. If you are not otherwise made aware of its happening, it is unlikely that the occurrence will occupy a place in your conscious mind. If that is true then the event cannot distract you from another activity or task with which you are occupied.

It is important that individual workers be shielded from inadvertent distraction made possible by their being able to observe activities and occurrences with which they have no concern except human curiosity. The same people need to be screened to separate them from activities in which they do have an interest or responsibility but do not need to be involved except at specific times for specific reasons.

Most, if not all, humans have natural desires such as curiosity, suspicion, and the desire to be included. At times these tendencies and traits are useful and productive. When brought into play incidentally in the workplace where there is no actual need or benefit for the individual's involvement or interest, the same characteristics become distractions and need to be prevented in the interest of productivity and profit.

Distraction through the sense of sight is relatively easy to prevent. It is accomplished on a daily basis by the use of private offices, particularly those with no windows, or with windows and closed blinds, and with doors that remain closed. To paraphrase Abraham Lincoln, this idea works for all of the people some of the time and for some of the people all of the time, but it does not work for all of the people all of the time.

Since most workers do not have private offices, it is necessary and desirable to provide freedom from sight distractions using sight barriers in another manner.

Free-Standing Screens

The use of free-standing screens is one method of accomplishing visual shielding for individual workstations. If a visual barrier was all that is necessary, this is by far the least expensive method to accomplish that goal. This type of screen is available in a wide selection of widths, heights, materials, finishes, and configurations; straight panels are available from all sources, and a few manufacturers produce curved panels.

The surfaces of some free-standing screens are tackable. They can be used as tackboards for notes and reference materials that are held in place by push pins or thumbtacks. Usually the tackable surfaces have a reduced ability to absorb sound. There are free-standing screens that do attenuate sound and still others that absorb sound and still allow you to use the surface for attaching reference materials. Any time a sound absorbing surface is made dense enough to hold tacks, it will lose part of its sound-absorbing quality. More about this later.

There are free-standing screens available that will support a limited number of storage units, usually shelves. Frequently the use of these storage units dictates screen size and layout. In other words, if you want to use the shelves that are available as a component, and the shelves are available only in a 36 inch (914 mm) length, the panels very often will have to be 36 inches (914 mm) wide as well.

Advantages. Free-standing screens give you the ability to disrupt sight lines, preventing inadvertent sight distraction.

Free-standing screens, depending on their materials and finishes, provide varying degrees of sound attenuation to help reduce distraction caused by sounds in the workplace.

Free-standing screens may or may not provide tackability for displaying notes and reference material.

Free-standing screens are readily portable. This fact makes the screens easy to relocate. This point alone gives free-standing screens the highest degree of flexibility relative to both initial installation and future reconfiguration. Since free-standing screens require no other furniture or parts for support, they may be located anywhere that you have the space to put them.

Disadvantages. Free-standing screens normally serve only as sight barriers; most have limited sound-absorbing capability.

Free-standing screens have extremely limited or no vertical storage options.

Free-standing screens usually have some type of supporting feet projecting from either side of the screen. Depending on the design of the supports, these may create a tripping hazard for people walking along the screens.

Some free-standing screens have loose-fitting or poorly fitting connectors attaching support feet to screens, making it difficult to align screens properly. Since free-standing screens are relatively light in weight, allowing ease of movement, they can easily get out of alignment, as well. This causes an uneven configuration, which for many is unacceptable. Most free-standing screens do not have leveling adjustments that allow you to compensate for unevenness in the floor. This contributes vertical unevenness to the alignment problems already described.

SOUND BARRIERS

In any organization there exists the need for various kinds of privacy. There are invariably papers, books, and other documents that should be seen only by the eyes of those who are authorized to see or use them. There are many conversations that must remain confidential and not be heard by anyone other than those for which the message is intended.

Unfortunately the materials that surround most areas in the workplace are not conducive to providing the kind of confidential protection needed from either inadvertant discovery or outright spying. Average walls and partitions found in most offices are usually two sheets of material separated by an air space. This construction is perfectly adequate as a sight barrier, particularly if there are doors to close and secure. When it comes to confidential conversations, however, this standard partition is virtually no barrier at all.

Sound travels through most materials with little trouble. In addition, sound travels through the tiniest passages between parts of the partition materials; through cracks around the edges, tops, and bottom of doors and windows; and through electric switch and outlet boxes that have been placed back-to-back by an electrician while the partition was being constructed. Sound will even find its way over the top of the partition, between the base of the partition and the floor and between the end of the partition and the wall or other partition to which it abuts.

Even when an effort is made to stop the passage of confidential messages through surrounding walls and partitions, the result is usually far from successful. The most frequently used method is to place a sound-absorbing material into the airspace of the partition between the surface sheets of material. While the sound-absorbing material will reduce the sound and soften it a bit, it will not stop the sound penetration through the various passages that exist in every screen, partition, and wall.

Another method of enclosing offices and other workstations is to use acoustical screens and acoustical, movable, full-height partitions. Many such products boast very high laboratory ratings for retarding and reducing sound passage. It should be noted, however, that the test data apply to an area of the screen or partition taken from the acoustical portion of the panel only. This sample is then sealed into an opening in a masonry wall. Sound is generated on one side of the wall while a microphone on the opposite side of the wall records whatever sound penetrates the sample. The difference in the sound level on the two sides of the wall determines the rating.

The test described is a legitimate test of the panel material. To my knowledge it is impossible to duplicate this condition in the workplace using the screens or panels in the manner for which they are designed.

We can be assured that sound will not penetrate our surrounding enclosure if we construct our area entirely of thick concrete, or line the walls with lead and have no doors, windows, or other openings into the area. Although this may provide virtually soundproof surroundings, as a practical matter it will make a very poor workstation; and face-to-face communication will be impossible.

It might be appropriate to point out that what we are considering here is the security of most standard white-collar operations. We are not considering corporate spying or sabotage, for such is the domain of those who specialize in security of another type. Although much of what we propose herein, relative to confidentiality, can help to foil those from outside the organization whose sole purpose is to steal company secrets, or in other ways hamper or take unfair advantage of the company, what we are primarily dealing with is security regarding payroll and other personnel information, corporate strategy timetables, and who is to be promoted and who is not. So much for what cannot be done about confidentiality in the workspace.

LEAK PREVENTION

Without resorting to desperate solutions such as walling ourselves in, there is a means of accomplishing confidentiality in the workplace that is quite simple and relatively inexpensive to install. The technique is known as electronic sound masking (ESM).

Electronic Sound Masking

It has been appropriately said that it is better to have no ESM at all rather than to have a bad one. It sometimes appears, however, that there may be more bad ones than good ones.

An electronic sound masking system consists of one or more sound generators, one or more amplifiers, and the appropriate speakers. As long as the system is adequately masking the sounds of the workspace, it can be said that the less obvious the system is the more successful it is. A good ESM will not intrude by calling attention to itself. If an ESM is distracting, then it becomes part of the problem and can never provide the solution expected and so necessary.

There are various kinds of ESM available. Each generates some kinds of electronic sound, amplifies it, and sends it over speakers throughout the workspace. Frequencies that are used to make up the masking sound can serve as an irritant and distraction if not properly designed and selected. It is therefore very important to choose masking units with care. On the marketplace you can purchase white noise, pink noise, variable noise, and assorted other noises. White noise is rather high pitched, resembles the sound of escaping steam, and like any high-frequency sound, can be quite irritating. Pink noise is of a lower pitch or frequency and is somewhat similar to the sounds one hears that are caused by the fast moving air of a heating or cooling system as it passes through a grill or diffuser. Pink noise, although not as potentially irritating as white noise, can still be improved on. Variable noise units allow for user adjustment of the frequency and volume. Like the battle of the thermostat, what satisfies one individual irritates another and becomes a distraction for that reason. Further, the speakers for adjustable units are usually located openly in the spaces to be masked, and proper dispersion of the sound is virtually impossible.

To be successful, the sound sources of the ESM must not be discernible. The sound sources I am referring to are the speakers where the masking sound is introduced into the workspace. Also the dispersion should be such that as you proceed through an ESM conditioned space the sound must be part of the ambiance, not louder or softer as you move from one part of the area to another.

The ESM that we recommend is made up of individual self-contained units, each with its own sound generator and speaker. The reason for this is that when one of the units is not operating, although this seldom occurs, the remainder of the units continues to mask the area until the fault can be corrected.

The correct ESM produces a sound that parallels the speech curve. When this sound is introduced into the space at a volume approximately 20 decibels lower than normal speech volume, proper electronic masking of the workspace occurs. The distracting air-borne noise irritants are no longer distracting. The telephones, the typewriters, and the copiers all seem to fade into some distant area, too far away to be noticed. The conversations become unintelligible and soft, if very near, and disappear altogether if they are as much as 15 feet away. Normal conversation, however, can be conducted as usual, but without the previous distractions. Confidential conversations in offices and conference areas will remain just that. Confidential conversations in open plan type manager and supervisor workstations can also remain confidential, if the dividers are of good acoustical construction and are surrounding the workstation on four sides.

It is important that the ESM for your workspace be planned and designed by a good acoustical consultant. As part of the fee the consultant will tune the entire installation to be certain that the space is functioning as designed.

Like the other elements of this productivity improvement system the electronic masking system is an important part. Also like the other elements it is cost effective with a short payback period.

LIGHTING

Each of the elements that go to make up the interior solution are important because each contributes significantly to optimizing the interior environment. As might be expected correct lighting makes a very important contribution inasmuch as inadequate lighting can cause both sensory distraction and fatigue.

As the lighting for your project is being designed, many factors will be considered and evaluated. Among these factors are

1. What kinds of work are to be performed in the area. Are reading and/or writing tasks required.
2. Quality of reading materials to be worked with. Is the contrast between what is to be read and the surface on which it is printed, typed, or written sufficient. If not, higher light levels are required.
3. How fast the work must be accomplished and what degree of accuracy is required? Again the need is for light levels that are sufficient for the speed and accuracy required by the tasks to be performed.
4. The ages of the individuals to be performing the work. As we age our ability to see clearly diminishes. We will still be able to see to perform the work, but the light level may need to be a bit higher.

CONDITIONED AIR

Air that fills the workplace and that we breathe is ideally the appropriate combination of ambiant air and fresh air from the outside of the building. Building codes required that the air in occupied buildings be completely changed several times per hour. In addition, the temperature and humidity of the air should be in the comfort zone for most individuals.

Distribution and Return

Different workers, because of their individual physiological makeup, have different needs relative to a temperature that makes them feel comfortable. Furthermore that temperature is not always the same for a particular person.

There are air distribution systems available on the market today that allow air temperature and volume to be adjusted at each workstation by the individual who occupies it. Other systems have adjustable fans to increase air movement between workstations for an added degree of control and comfort by the individual white-collar worker.

Electronic filtering of the interior air for the workplace will go a long way toward removing allergens and other impurities that can contribute to illness and lost productivity. The number of smoke-free workplace environments is continually increasing as is their contribution to the wellness factor for all workers. Where smoking is allowed, more aggressive steps should be taken to exhaust, freshen, and filter the air, again to protect the health of all employees.

Live Plants Contribute to Clean Air

Because of its need to perfect viable living environments in permanent space stations the National Aeronautics and Space Administration (NASA) conducts many experiments concerning every aspect of living in an artificial environment.

Studies conducted by NASA have shown that living plants remove quantities of carbon dioxide from the air and replace it with water vapor and oxygen. More important is the fact that certain types of green and flowering plants can, after converting certain poisons in the air to plant food, return to the air, in place of the contaminate, more oxygen. What poisons are in the air of the buildings we inhabit? Formaldehyde, benzene, and carbon monoxide are examples of poisons that can be reduced by growing live plants in the workplace environment.

The gases mentioned are introduced into the workplace interior in a number of different ways. In his book *Office Hazards—How Your Job Can Make You Sick* Joel Makower writes,

> In offices, the biggest source of CO [carbon monoxide] is outside air, resulting from automobile exhaust being sucked into building ventilation systems. Thus buildings in downtown areas or along busy roadways are the ones most affected by this problem—but not exclusively. In a number of instances, underground garages and loading docks have generated high levels of carbon monoxide, which then filter up into offices.*

Formaldehyde is a chemical poison that may be released into any interior environment from a variety of commonly used building materials, and benzene is a contaminate that is contained in cleaning solvents and solutions, as

---

*Excerpted with permission from "Office Hazards: How Your Job Can Make You Sick" by Joel Makower (Washington, D.C.: Tilden Press Inc., 1981). Copyright © 1981 by Tilden Press Inc.

well as in chemicals that are used in some kinds of office equipment. Although the use of live plants in the workplace will not totally solve the problem of contaminates in the ambiant air of the workplace, tests by NASA indicate that substantial reductions in interior air pollution can be achieved.

Plants that have been tested by NASA and found to be effective in processing and lowering the levels of pollutants from the air of interior spaces include (1) Philodendron, (2) Gerbera Daisy, (3) Chrysanthemum, (4) Spathiphyllum, (5) Dracaena Warnecki, and (6) Dracaena Marginata. According to NASA, the Philodendron, in small spaces, can reduce atmospheric toxic levels of benzene and formaldehyde more than 87% over a 24-hour time period. When testing with only benzene, the Gerbera Daisy lowered the level of this carcinogen 69% in a like 24-hour span of time. Of six plants listed above, the remaining four while scoring less than the Gerbera Daisy, were quite effective in reducing the toxic levels of benzene. Additional plants are being tested. At NASA, Dr. B. C. Wolverton, the investigator in charge of environmental research, asks rhetorically, "If you put plants in buildings will it help improve air quality? We say, from our tests, yes indeed. The more foliage, the healthier the environment is going to be."

We referred in the preceding section to the problems created by tobacco smoke. Joel Makower, in *Office Hazards*, reports further concerning particulates:

> Tobacco smoke itself contains nearly 3,000 compounds—among them ammonia, benzene, formaldehyde, propane, acetylene, hydrogen sulphide and methane—and the smoke's presence produces carbon monoxide, which interferes with the oxygen-carrying ability of the blood. Moreover, cigarette smoke picks up and transports particulate matter, including dust, spores, fungi and particles of loose fibers, such as asbestos.*

Later he writes,

> Particulates. Any substances small enough to be inhaled into the body—dust, soot, or ash, for example—have potential for harm, since they can become deposited in the lungs. The biggest problems come from cigarette smoke, which has the tendency to gather up other particulates in the air and allow them to hang there for hours when they might otherwise escape through the ventilation exhaust systems. . . . cigarette smoke can increase particulate levels by 10 to 100 times.*

This is another incentive for making the workplace smoke-free.

---

*Excerpted with permission from "Office Hazards: How Your Job Can Make You Sick" by Joel Makower (Washington, D.C.: Tilden Press Inc., 1981). Copyright © 1981 by Tilden Press Inc.

SURFACE ACOUSTICAL TREATMENT

It is desirable to reduce the reflectivity of large surfaces of the workspace by using finish materials that are absorptive and that will attenuate sounds that contact them. It is important that the materials used primarily absorb the higher frequency sounds, where more of the deterrent elements occur, and to allow the lower frequencies to be less affected, these being more useful as long as they are not too loud.

Ceilings

The two largest horizontal surfaces in any workplace are the floor and the ceiling. Each is the approximate size of the other. The two surfaces are parallel and opposite to each other, and these two surfaces can be a large part of the workplace aural problem, bouncing sounds to each other and then reflecting those same sounds again and again until it is extremely difficult to think about anything but the noise. All that is required is for these surfaces to present hard reflective materials as a finish.

Conversely these same two horizontal surfaces, when constructed of and/or finished with the appropriate materials can attenuate any sound that contacts its surface, absorbing some parts, allowing some sound parts to pass through, and reflecting other sound parts back into the space from which it came. The sound that is reflected to the other surface is much weaker, drained of its energy, and will soon be reduced to virtually no sound at all. As such the sound is not, nor can it become, a deterrent.

As we stated above it is important with all acoustical materials that absorbtion is greater in the high and medium range frequencies and less in the low frequencies. It is also desirable to have some type of backing to retard sound passage through the material. The highest reasonable light reflectivity for the surface finish is another characteristic that must be included.

Walls, Columns, and Partitions

The most used and appropriate treatments for these types of surfaces involve glass fiber matt adhered to the wall and faced with acoustically transparent fabric. Acoustically transparent means that the fabric allows the sound to pass through with little or no effect, on the sound, to the glass fiber absorption material, which actually attenuates the sound. Another material that is not only durable but that is also attractive and relatively inexpensive is broadloom carpet. There are also several acoustical wall coverings on the market that have sound-attenuating value. Any material that diffuses and/or absorbs the sounds that contact it contributes to the reduction of aural distraction in the workplace.

Screens

Acoustical screens, by their location, and if they are tall enough, will also be visual barriers. As long as the material of the screen is opaque it will serve well as such a sight barrier. The screen, however, as a vertical surface in the workplace, must be treated acoustically. Whether the screens are free-standing or are part of a systems furniture installation matters little when it comes to the need for acoustical treatment. The same glass fiber material that I mentioned relative to walls, partitions, columns, and so on, applies to screens. As a matter of fact, all of the materials previously mentioned for use on vertical surfaces are available for use and are used to provide sound absorption and attenuation for screens and systems furniture panels.

Windows and Glass Interior Walls

The deterrent reduction solution relating to windows, borrow lights, or transparent walls in conference rooms, offices, computer rooms, and workmodules, whether made of glass or other glazing materials, while essentially the same, is different. In each, the goal is to prevent something from passing from one side of the glazing material to the other to the greatest extent possible. For windows in the exterior walls of the structure, the solution normally involves the control of solar radiation and glare. The solution for interior glass, whether a borrow light, a side light, or a transparent wall normally involves the installation of an adjustable, visual barrier to prevent someone from seeing through the transparent wall or opening.

It is not my intention to discuss extensively the subject of window management, as it relates to the control of solar radiation and energy conservation. There are, however, certain aspects of this specialty that impact on white-collar productivity and the white-collar workplace. Two numbers, the shading coefficient of the glazing assembly, and the openness factor of draperies, shades, or blinds may affect how comfortable an individual is in the workplace under certain conditions.

The first number, shading coefficient, indicates the difference in the solar heat gain, shaded and not shaded. Stated another way, the shading coefficient reflects the difference between the solar radiation that contacts the outside of the glazing material in a windowed area and the solar radiation that actually enters the space itself. Clear glass and no shading devices of any kind will produce a shading coefficient of 1.0. Shading options range from exterior shading devices, such as awnings and automatic movable, or fixed shades, to coated and tinted glazing materials, to interior shading devices such as blinds, either vertical or horizontal, shades, or draperies.

If workers are located in areas that receive the sun's rays and the glazing assembly has a shading coefficient of 0.30, those individuals will still receive 30 percent of the sun that they would if they were setting on a sunny beach. Cool conditioned air aside those workers may feel uncomfortable even though the air around them is at a comfortable temperature.

Although it is ideal to intercept the solar radiation while it is outside the building and keep it there, in most instances some of it will pass through the glazing material and will become part of the cooling loads for the building. The addition of interior shading devices, preferably light in color, will reflect more of the solar radiation back through the glazing and into the atmosphere. Although the process is more involved than that brief description, this is essentially what takes place.

The other number, called the openness factor, relates to the amount of open area that exists in the material of various shading devices. For example, if the yarn in a shade fabric occupies 70 percent of its area, then the balance of the area, 30 percent, constitutes the space between the strands of yarn. Solar radiation can come through this space. Just like the shading coefficient, the solar radiation that penetrates the shading device is the same solar radiation that will burn your skin at the beach or on the golf course, although diminished by the shading material. The openness factor applies to any fabric used for shading. It may be in a drapery, it may be fabric in a vertical blind, or it may be the fabric of a shade. If the glazing material is clear, the openness factor of the shading material tells you how much solar radiation will come through. If the glazing assembly has a shading coefficient, then the material of the interior shading device will provide protection in addition to the shading coefficient.

Glass walls are expensive. And if you are going to have a functional room with a glass wall, you must have some kind of visual control device, such as vertical blinds, on the inside of that wall, as well. If one is willing to pay the price, both the original cost of the glass and the cost to install a visual control device, there is no reason for not having a glass wall. All of this can be avoided, however, by either not having glass walls or panels, or by fitting such glass areas with visual control devices.

In addition to acting as a visual screen, vertical blinds will provide an acoustical barrier to intercept, divert, and break up sound which contacts its various surfaces and prevent direct reflection of the sound back into the area. As long as the blinds are not drawn, the device will work in either the open or closed position.

Floors

There is a particular need for acoustical treatment of floor surfaces. A hard surface floor finish, such as hardwood, terrazzo, or marble, will normally contribute greatly to aural distraction. The reason has to do with what is known as impact noise, which is mentioned elsewhere in this book. Impact noise results when one hard object contacts another hard object with force. It may be a contact that is accidental, when an object is dropped and falls to the floor, or it may be intentional, when someone is walking across the floor. Each time that person's heel strikes the floor, particularly if the heel of their shoe is of a hard or a relatively hard material, an impact sound will occur and will be heard by those within a certain radius of distance. From experience I can assure you that this will provide a distraction that is hard to ignore. The obvious treatment at best is carpet. Not only will the carpet help to absorb all of the ambient sounds of the workplace, it will virtually eliminate all but the loudest impact noises, which are usually caused by large falling objects and which do not, in most workplaces, occur very often. Modular carpet or carpet tiles are particularly efficient in attenuating impact noises, in addition to having other advantages.

THE MOVABLE ELEMENT

The single greatest opportunity for increasing productivity in the Beta Sector comes through the design and configuration of individual workstations.

Workstations

The term workstation, like so many others lately, is used incorrectly by advertising and marketing people as a way to sell their products. As a result of such usage the population is sometimes confused by a language that has more than a single meaning for too many words, as it is. Architecture has nothing to do with computers except to use them as a tool, as would any other discipline or business; and workstation does not refer to one particular piece of electronic hardware. And it matters not how wonderfully indescribable that particular product is, what it can do, or how fast or or how well. One piece of equipment or furniture, or 20 pieces, does not make up a workstation. A workstation is territory.

Think of the the workplace as a town or city. All of the white-collar workspaces together go to make up this town. The different departments represent different burroughs or districts. The individual workstations represent individual houses where people live and the aisles become the streets and avenues of the city. The smallest subdivision of this "city," like most cities, is the individual plot or residence. So it is with the white-collar workplace, except that the smallest subdivision is the individual workstation.

The workstation is the space assigned to each individual from one end of the organization to the other. In some instances the space assigned is part of a larger space and is shared by many other white-collar workers. The individual spaces may be divided by screens, or the only definition of the space may be the desk and chair space allotted to the individual assigned to it.

The subject of workstations is presented in another part of this book. Although all of the elements of this profit improvement system are important and each contributes to the optimum solution for increasing white-collar productivity, the largest single contribution is to be made by the workstation and its work modules. The design of the workstation and the configuration of the workstation and its workmodule are major contributors to the well-being and the success or failure of every white-collar workplace; of importance is not only the orientation of each individual workstation, but how it relates to adjacent workstations as well. Each of these parts either makes a contribution to, or reduces the potential success of any productivity improvement program.

If, for any reason, management is limited to the use of a single element of this entire program, the properly designed and configured workstation is the element to choose. Most of the system furniture currently in use today can be modified to gain the benefits described herein, although not without cost. When that is not possible or desirable, new system furniture can provide a very short payback, allowing quick recovery of the investment necessary to accomplish the improvement.

Refurbished Systems Furniture

In the late 1970s and the 1980s a different kind of business came into existence and grew. These were companies that buy up used systems furniture, repaint it, replace the fabric, and replace missing parts. In some cases worn or defective parts are also replaced. These companies also approach organizations who are planning to buy new systems furniture and suggest that their old furniture or systems furniture be replaced with refurbished systems furniture. The refurbisher then takes the organization's old furniture as part payment for refurbished furniture that they purchase.

The quality of work done by these firms varies from one firm to the next, as in any segment of the service sector. In each situation, however, there is no question about the fact that you are buying used merchandise. Like the automobiles you see on the lot of the used car agency, they look great, and although systems furniture has relatively few moving and electrical components, these are susceptible to wear.

Some refurbishers relace worn or defective parts and some do not. If you feel that you must buy from a refurbisher, try to be certain as to what you are getting.

As I have pointed out previously, with the increased productivity available to you as a result of workplace optimization through work in the Beta Sector, all of the money you spend can be recovered within a short period of time. That makes it possible for your organization to own new systems furniture and the warrantees that go with them, and makes it unnecessary to settle for used systems or conventional furniture. Again, depending on the size of your company and market conditions, it may even be possible to actually buy new furniture for less than the cost of refurbished furniture from a quality refurbisher.

5

AESTHETICS VS. FUNCTION

Unless you are designing a monument such as Sarinen's Arch in St. Louis or The Washington Monument in Washington, D.C., the activity that takes place inside of a structure is the only justification for its existence. All too often, however, the functional aspects of the workplace are given only cursory attention, if they are not ignored completely.

VISUAL DESIGN VERSUS WORKPLACE FUNCTION

Space planning is almost entirely concerned with function, whereas the visual aspects of design make a functional contribution in addition to affording the pleasure of a pleasant aesthetic experience.

The functional aspects of a layout should not be subordinated to the aesthetic wishes of a secretary, a spouse, an interior designer, an architect, or anyone else. The inherent problems resulting from *design* suggestions contributed by associates, employees, and relatives result, many times, in horror stories almost too terrible to mention. With professionals, trading functional necessity or efficiency should not be tolerated. Such subordination is not necessary if a dual approach is followed throughout the design process of the project, with equal weight afforded to each discipline. Also, a sincere concern for both the functional success as well as the visual success of the completed project needs to exist in the mind of the planner and designer. This concern must exist continually as the work is being executed, if the project is to be totally successful.

It is important to realize and important to *know* that there is more to a successful workplace interior than a pleasant aesthetic experience. There are always tradeoffs to be made. An important point to remember, however, is that cost effectiveness is achieved to a far greater degree through the accommodation of functional need than can ever be achieved through the accommodation of excessive want for specific appearance. The truly successful planner and/or designer will manage to achieve both. The truly successful workplace interior will possess both.

It is not necessary to surrender the aesthetics of superior appearance to achieve a facility that provides superior performance. These qualities are not mutually exclusive. They can and should coexist and it is not necessary to give up one to have the other. Perhaps the redundancy of this paragraph will help to drive home the point that "A Facility Can Work Well and Still Be Outstanding Visually."

As an example, different designers have different tastes and preferences when it comes to selecting a ceiling board for a suspended, lay-in ceiling.

All ceiling boards have technical characteristics that determine how well each will perform to satisfy certain functional requirements, how well it acts as a fire barrier, and how well it reflects light. It has still other characteristics that determine what will happen to sounds that come in contact with it? How much of the sound it will let pass through? How much sound will it absorb and at what frequencies? How much of the sound that contacts it is reflected back into the space from which it originated?

Many designers will be more, if not totally, concerned with how the board will look when it is in place. A favorite board with many designers and architects is a type that has deep natural fissures. The board also has good acoustical properties for certain applications, appropriate fire protection qualities, but only fair light reflectivity. This type of board is used often in an inappropriate situation with the sole criterion applied being that of appearance.

CAVEAT EMPTOR: LET THE BUYER BEWARE

Many individuals who are payed by clients, businessmen who have retained the person or persons to perform a *design* service or services for their organization, either do not know how, or do not care enough to determine, what the client's functional needs and aesthetic desires really are. Still others, even if they do know what is needed functionally, are interested only in the visual aspects of the project and give little or no attention to, let alone provide solutions for the problems of productivity in the workplace. The same holds true for many individuals who are payed by their employers to design for the firm's clients. With that thought in mind, it seems rather certain that in all of the situations in which such conditions exists, the only opportunity for a successful outcome is by accident or coincidence.

During times of intense competition, in particular, most entrepreneurial types seeking ways to increase their share of the market offer more products and more service to their customers or clients. Interior design studios, space planning firms, architectural firms, and other consulting groups are businesses too. Like other businesses each strives to expand, to increase its potential revenue and profit.

Our (*specific product, specific service*) *will increase your white-collar productivity* (*tremendously, unbelievably, extraordinarily*). For a number of years these magic words have been used to sell every conceivable piece of electronic equipment, machine, and service. In some instances the claims are true. In other situations the promise of success is so dependent on specific conditions being true that if any part is not in place, or any variables are not exactly as prescribed, productivity results are greatly reduced and in some cases nonexistent. Understandably many businessmen and managers have become cynical and suspicious.

White-collar productivity improvement has become a *buzz word* that has been noticed by many people with something to sell. Included in that group are interior designers, space planners, architects, and many other consultants who know that productivity improvement of any kind is an ongoing goal of businesses everywhere. I have seen workplace after workplace in which projects with large fees were sold as a result of the seller's promise to deliver some percentage of increased productivity by some segment of, or the entire white-collar workforce. What was delivered was a rehash of the same old concepts, the same old layouts that have been around for more than 50 years.

In the December 1986 issue of *Architecture*, George Rand, at the time the associate dean of UCLA's graduate school of architecture and urban planning, in his article, *Whatever Happened to the Office of the Future?*, stated

> Despite the rapid rise in the use of office technology, we are left with a pretty parochial idea of the office space itself: a desk, a chair and a sidetable.*

Even when the professionals use systems furniture, the components are frequently selected to create the same desk, chair, and sidetable arrangement that George Rand refers to in his article. Why? Because most are giving little thought as to how to improve the work situation for the individual worker or the productivity for the organization. The interest, too often, is in *how great it will look*!

Aesthetics

How great it will look is extremely important. But before that look can be accomplished the consultant must know that it is vital to understand what management wants to communicate to people who enter their workplace. It is as important for the designer and/or architect to listen, to hear, and to be able to translate that information into a workplace that will communicate just such a message. Most often the message is very simple. *We are here, we know what we are doing, we will serve you well, your time and/or money will be well spent with our organization, and we want your visit to be remembered as a pleasant experience.*

More than one business owner or manager has set out on a national, and sometimes even international, quest to locate the type of interior wanted for his or her new offices. After having visited many installations, some of which

*From *Architecture* magazine, December 1986, © BPI Communications, Inc.

have won awards for their interior designs, and different offices with various styles of interior office design, these individuals often return discouraged, without having discovered what they were seeking. Although these officers probably have noted several parts of designs that they *kind of like*, they have not seen anything that they have a desire to duplicate.

An architect who, a number of years ago, was designing small churches related that when he would ask the parishioners, or the church building committee, if there was a particular style that they preferred for the design of the church exterior, he would often hear, "We just want it to look like a church." Although such a statement seems to have an obvious answer, such is not the case. It requires another question: "What does a church look like—to you?"

Although it is true that each of the members of the congregation agreed on a design declaration, it is also true that each had his or her own mental picture of what that meant. In many, if not all situations the architect also has a mental picture of that statement, and many times the architect's mental picture does not even come close to any of the pictures held by the individuals of the church constituency.

What was eventually determined by the church architect was that a vast majority of the people involved meant that to look like a church the design had to include a steeple. And the closer it was in appearance to a small colonial church that they remembered from their youth, or from a picture that they had seen somewhere, the better.

It is not easy for management to tell the architect or designer what they think they want their business workplace to look like, to be like, even to feel like as clients, customers, employees, and peers work in, or otherwise experience the space. This is not something that most businessmen do every day and therefore are not necessarily familiar or comfortable with the terms of the interiors, building parts, and systems to the same degree as the consultant. And, although management may throw in words that may seem to indicate a particular style or design direction, such words may not have the same meaning for the owner or manager as they do for the architect or designer.

The task of the architect/designer, relative to the interior design for the workplaces of an organization, is primarily to listen intently, both to what management is saying and to what management is not saying. There is much information contained in each. This is where the real skill of design comes into play. The designer must be able to know from what is communicated by management what is intended and what is desired, and be able to translate that knowledge into the design statement that will ultimately be presented by the organization to the world.

In other situations an architect/designer may hear what the business owner or corporate officer is saying, but feels that everyone would be better served by the designer's own ideas. An ego trip is seldom either sought or accepted willingly by anyone, and it is extremely presumptuous on the part of the designer. Any input by the officer is negated, and if the input is relative to something the individual feels very strongly about, may be taken as a direct affront.

I am reminded of a situation in which an architect, for whom I was providing consulting interior architectural services, lived through just such an experience. We had been commissioned to plan and design the corporate offices for a large holding corporation. The officer contact was the board chairman and he was quite easy to work with. During the first meeting, which I attended, he gave us an overview with his thoughts concerning the entire project. The particular floor we were discussing was to accommodate the senior executives of the corporation. The Chairman expounded on all aspects of the various elements to be located on this level, saving his own areas until last.

We were meeting in the Chairman's private conference area, which was furnished with furniture from a particular manufacturer. If we had not noticed the fact, it was soon to be pointed out to us by the Chairman. We then moved our meeting to his adjacent and connecting office. This area also was furnished exclusively with furniture from the same manufacturer, and that fact was likewise pointed out to us with glowing admiration by the Chairman. He went on to say that a great many of the furnishings for his residence were likewise by the same manufacturer.

Without ever saying he wanted to use any particular furniture in his new office and conference area he asked, "Do you understand what I am saying?" Each of us answered affirmatively. The meeting ended and we left.

I returned to my office and over a period of time completed the preliminary presentation, including plans and presentation boards for the project. A meeting was held a week prior to the presentation with the architect for whom I was consulting. I went over the presentation indicating all of the various items that we were recommending for use on the project. Everything was smooth sailing until we reached the Chairman's office, wherein I had indicated furniture by the manufacturer that he seemed to love so much, and as far as I was concerned, he had instructed us to use for his conference area and for his private office.

Although not insisting on changing the conference area, the architect said he wanted to change the private office furnishings to a different manufacturer, one often specified by architects and designers, and an excellent choice both in quality and design. The furniture was similarly priced. We discussed the previous conversation we had with the Chairman. I felt quite certain of the Chairman's intentions and that he would not be swayed. The architect indicated that he remembered the conversation, but believed that the officer would prefer the alternate furniture he wanted to use, once the Chairman saw it, but felt that he could convince him to use it in any case.

The documents and presentation materials were changed to reflect the alternate selections for the Chairman's private office and another meeting was scheduled. The second meeting proceeded without incident as the various offices and areas were presented and with the Chairman nodding his satisfaction and approval of each. The last two areas to be presented were the officer's own conference area and private office. As the architect began his description and recommendations for those two areas, the Chairman became uncharacteristically quiet and motionless. He slouched in his chair, something I had never seen him do before, and his face slowly changed to an expression of utter dissatisfaction. When the architect had finished his presentation, believing he had sold the client completely, the chairman rose from his chair, saying he would have to think about it, turned, went into his office, and closed the door behind him. The architect felt certain that the presentation had been completely successful. We left with absolutely nothing approved, however.

The next day, early, I received a call at my office from the Chairman. He asked me if I could meet him the following day in Chicago. I said I would and asked if the architect was to be there also? He indicated that it would only be the two of us, and asked that I meet him at the showroom of the manufacturer whose furniture he presently had in his office, conference area, and residence. When I arrived at the showroom we went directly into the manager's office, which had been turned over to the Chairman for our meeting. This is a courtesy extended only to very good customers, which was obviously the way the Chairman was viewed, and in fact actually was.

Once alone in the office the Chairman said he would like me to tell him what I thought he wanted for his areas of the corporate executive offices. I answered that I believed he wanted his areas furnished completely with furniture from the manufacturer in whose showroom offices we were meeting. The Chairman paused for a few moments, then smiled a very large smile, and said, "You know, I thought no one was listening to me. Take care of it will you."

Once again the documents and presentation materials were changed. Another meeting was scheduled and began by presenting the Chairman's office and conference area, each of which was completely furnished with furniture from the manufacturer of his choice. With but one very small adjustment the furniture package for the entire floor was approved. After the Chairman had departed the architect commented, "That's fine. Whatever he wants."

Ego is seldom sought by business owners unless an architect or designer is being retained because of a reputation or an ability to produce outlandish designs that attract attention. Most organizations look to ad agencies for this sort of statement, not for their buildings or interior designs, but for media advertising. Although the ideas and the design may be novel, it may also be tiring in a relatively short time. If an ad campaign has lost its attractiveness it can easily be replaced. The same approach is not generally feasible with a corporate interior or a building. In a few instances, however, corporations have had to bite the bullet and pay for another new interior or different systems furniture to overcome excessive operating costs associated with a particular design or product.

The key to success in corporate architecture and interior design work is information: to have it, to translate it, and to use it wisely. Listen intently and gather the information you need.

Function

I have yet to hear the owner or manager of a business say about a new facility, or an existing facility for that matter, "I really don't care whether this office works functionally or not, I just want it to look great." There is no doubt in my mind that such a statement has been made, a number of times, probably. In the past, correct office function was often assumed as a given. That, what it is, it is, and there was little to be done to improve it; often little or no thought was given to it at all.

Sophisticated owners and managers of today realize that effort must be made to extract every facet of advantage from the function of their workplaces. If their organization is to thrive, and if they are to obtain maximum profit dollars from the profit potential that is available to them, it is necessary for them to maximize their workplaces.

To properly plan and design a workplace it is necessary to have as much information as can be reasonably obtained about the organization, about its management, and, most importantly, about the people who do the bulk of the work and about the work that they do.

One key to successful workplace optimization is information. It is important to know how the organization is operating *now*, not how management thinks it is operating based on a myriad of directives, memos, and other communication documents that have been distributed over the years since the company was founded, purchased, acquired, reorganized, or whatever (see Chapter 12).

Another key is flexibility. Rigidity is the format of the past and should be completely unacceptable now. There is absolutely no way to know with any degree of certainty what the necessary organizational composition of a dynamic company will be 6 months, 1 year, or 2 years from now. The prudent workplace will allow for change, on very short notice—change with a minimum of disruption and distraction in the workplace. Remember that *Distraction* in the workplace means *Subtraction* from the bottom line.

An organization that is not able to respond to the need for rearranging workstations as the result of new group alignments will also see that fact reflected in its bottom line.

A PAIN AT BEST

Interior designers, architects, space planners, and other consultants often seem to arrive on the scene prepared to perform whatever chore is needed to save the businesspeople and their organizations from themselves. In fact, no matter how capable the individual professional is, and regardless of how accomplished their people are, the tasks that they will necessarily perform for the client will be disruptive to the client's employees and hence to the client's operation.

Every change an organization makes is disruptive to the operation to some degree. The more of the client's workers involved, either directly or indirectly, the greater the disruption and the greater the cost, much of which is never accounted for. It is easy for professionals to view the design process with its associated activities, such as construction and moving, as part of the client's business operation. It is important for all players, consultant, and client to remember that the sooner the design process is completed, the construction finished, and the furniture installed or reconfigured, the quicker the client and the client's organization can get back to what they do in the conduct of their business. The design process with its attendant activities are not part of that business, only the results are, for better or worse. The design process, for the business, is a pain at best.

6

FURNITURE AND EQUIPMENT

Furniture and equipment are the stuff of workmodules. Workmodules are what keep workstations from being just empty spaces, and workstations are where individual workers make or break a business organization.

THE DESK—THE WORKHORSE

The rectangular table or desk has been with us since the days of the Egyptian Pharoahs, and with very little change. What is now known as the standard 30 by 60 inch double pedestal desk has for several decades been the workhorse of the office force and has served quite well. This period of service was, during a time when office workers received relatively low salaries and made up a small percentage of the total workforce. Efforts to make productivity gains in the white-collar sector were limited, at best, and such efforts were generally given a low priority.

The situation has changed. Today more than 60 percent of the workforce is employed in white-collar jobs. With average white-collar salaries, including benefits, frequently exceeding $20,000 annually for many companies, there is quite an incentive to reduce operating costs by any means available. Increasing white-collar productivity is an effective way to accomplish such a goal.

The time is long overdue for the workhorse to be put out to pasture! The rectangular desk has never equipped a workstation for efficient work production by the individual, and it is not conducive to cost-effective productivity.

Consider that the desk that is normally specified for use in the white-collar workplace has only straight lines. Consider further that the individuals who are expected to use it have no straight lines at all, and whose ranges of motion for their heads, arms, and eyes are circular, not straight. On most rectangular desks a sizable portion of the primary worksurface cannot be comfortably reached by a majority of those expected to use it, and the location of storage below the worksurface makes its use excessively time consuming.

To say that a rectangular desk of any size cannot be used to perform white-collar work is obviously not true. The truth is that having workers use such desks has become an expensive way to have the job done. If you are interested in achieving maximum improvement of your white-collar productivity potential, keeping your workers behind rectangular desks is not the way to accomplish your goal.

SYSTEMS FURNITURE—THE NEW WORKHORSE

So what happens when the desks are taken away? When conventional furniture is eliminated from the options available in the marketplace today about all that is left is systems furniture of one kind or another.

One of the problems with such furniture, at this point in time, is overchoice. There are many furniture systems available and each has its own advantages and disadvantages. With each system there are trade-offs and although none has all of the features necessary to produce maximum efficiency, most of the systems being manufactured currently do provide a base from which to work. It should be noted that although systems furniture is more expensive initially, if correctly used it is also cost effective.

Any organization honestly seeking the workspace that is most conducive to productivity improvement *must* invest in systems furniture. Also, if such a goal is to be achieved, individual workstations must provide the following characteristics:

1. Flexibility: Flexibility is extremely important. Any business should be able to easily respond as the need for organizational realignment, growth, or downsizing necessitates reconfiguration of the workplace.
2. Adjustability: Adjustability allows each workstation to be tailored, as necessary, to accommodate the individual, and his or her storage, reference surfaces, worksurfaces, and equipment needs, as determined by their job description.
3. Deterrent Reduction: The individual workstations must contribute to the minimization or the elimination of as many of the deterrents to white-collar productivity as possible.

The installation of systems furniture in your white-collar workplace does not, in and of itself, ensure increased individual productivity or increased profit. Systems furniture will provide a flexible tool to be used by workers as they perform the tasks required of them. Systems furniture, when properly designed and configured, will eliminate many common fatigue factors found in workplaces everywhere. System furniture that meets the goals listed above will contribute to the reduction and removal of distraction.

Beware of designers, consultants, and marketing people who promise to increase productivity but who actually have little knowledge of, or interest in, the functional aspects of your operation. Also, remember that you do not have to give up a pleasing appearance to have a workplace that is cost effective.

Like any other single part of the solution to white-collar productivity improvement, systems furniture alone will not solve all of the problems. If improperly used the system may actually cause more problems than it solves. Systems furniture, planned to accomplish functional goals that result in increased productivity and that possess the characteristics listed above, can be one of the most effective tools to use in achieving an increased productivity potential.

Any organization now equipped with conventional desks and chairs, that hopes to accomplish the maximum productivity potential in their white-collar workplace, needs to invest in a properly designed systems furniture installation. Those who have a systems furniture installation that is not delivering the productivity gains promised need to invest in the redesign of their existing system to gain the benefits inherent in the systems furniture concept.

WORKSTATION SEATING

One area in which we have been frustrated by the limited productivity improvements results that could be delivered is that of the workstation chair. The chair is clearly one of the most important, if not the most important piece of equipment the white-collar worker uses.

The deterrent to productivity here is sensory, inasmuch as the individual worker comes into physical contact with the chair, and the sense of touch detects comfort or discomfort that is relayed to the individual's brain and distracts or does not distract, as the case may be. Another deterrent is fatigue. Since dealing with adjusting one's body throughout the work period is a fatigue factor as well as a discomfort associated with sitting, fatigue will be cumulative and inasmuch as it cannot be eliminated totally, needs to be reduced as much as possible.

My opinion is that, historically, most chair manufacturers have been remiss in not producing chairs with greater ranges of adjustments so as to accommodate, more comfortably, a larger segment of the workforce. Although many chair manufacturers have made advances by adding or including various types of adjustments, the ranges of those adjustments often are insufficient to accommodate people in the fifth percentile whose size should be accommodated and virtually never in the first percentile. Only very recently has much attention been given to solving the most prevalent problems of the back and other physiological problems caused by improper sitting for extended periods of time.

Management has been plagued by productivity loss due to workers' back problems. Such ailments constitute the second largest cause of employee absenteeism, accounting for an average of 0.83 days per worker per year, according to the U.S. Department of Health and Human Services.

Although less than one day per year per employee may not seem like much of a time loss, such loss is only the tip of the iceberg. A 1981 study by the Technical University of Berlin, Germany, showed that of the group of visual display terminal users surveyed, 43 percent of those performing clerical tasks sought treatment for relief of back ailments. All of the group were in the 31–40 year age bracket, and 60 percent of those performing data or text input tasks sought treatment for the same type of back problems. An additional 30 percent of the group examined felt varying degrees of discomfort, but did not seek medical treatment.

The nearly one day per year per person lost due to back ailments accounts for days where the employee is actually absent from the workplace. It does not account for the countless hours spent by individuals as they attempt to relieve discomfort by standing, stretching, taking a trip to the restroom, to the water fountain, or an otherwise unnecessary trip to to the supply room or mailroom. When our back gives us pain, we try to ease it by any and every means possible. Such attempts at solving our backaches take time; and since each such solution is only temporary, it must be repeated over and over again during the course of a work period totaling large, unrecorded losses of productivity.

For years we have been instructed from childhood on to *sit up straight.* Such a command refers to an individual sitting erect with a right angle formed between the torso and the thighs. Such a position of *attention* is now considered by most as the only correct sitting posture. Such a position can be maintained for only a short period of time, however, before discomfort begins to set in, requiring an adjustment to the position.

As early as 1884, Dr. F. Staffel, a German orthopedic surgeon, warned of the problems associated with individuals required by their jobs to stay seated for long periods of time. He stated that to assume the position, even for a short period of time, required using sets of muscle against other sets of muscles. Dr. Staffel was well aware, even in 1884, that the right angle *sit up straight* position was impossible to maintain for very long inasmuch as it causes excessive pressure on the intervertebral discs, which in turn causes back ailments and pain.

Dr. Staffel also noted that a horse riding saddle would make a far better seat for a working person than a chair that has essentially a right angle between the seat and back. Regardless of the information contained in Dr. Staffel's writings and other authoritative reports, nearly a century would pass before a 1977 report by Dr. A.C. Mandel of Denmark caused three European manufacturers to design, develop, and manufacture seating devices to meet the physiological needs of what Dr. Mandel refers to as Homo Sedens or Seated Man.

As a critic I have often stated that "I can only get so excited about a chair," and as *new* chair after *new* chair has been introduced to the marketplace, my attitude has almost always been ambivalent at best. Not much was happening functionally; and problems were certainly not being solved, in my opinion.

Let us consider for a while what does happen physiologically when an individual changes from a standing position to a seated one? Let us go back to where it all begins. When we are born, our spine has no particular shape and assumes whatever position our body is put into. It is not until we are small children, walking and running, and our spine must assume a shape that will balance the body, that what is often described as the double "S" curve is formed (see Figure 6.1). This shape serves two principal functions. First, it balances the body so that it will remain upright while supporting the weight of the torso, and second, it acts as a spring of sorts, which can handle the jolting that occurs when we run or jump, without damaging the spine or other parts of the body.

As we grow and our bodies develop, the double "S" shape becomes the normal balanced position of the various vertebrae that together make up the spine. In this balanced position the spaces between the vertebrae are adjusted so that the substance between the vertebrae, which is known as the intervertebral disc, fits properly and without undue or excess pressure from the adjacent vertebrae.

So far so good. We might add here that the intervertebral discs are not entirely cleansed by the blood. In addition, these very important segments of the spine are cleaned, as we walk or otherwise move our back, pelvis, and legs, much like you would clean a sponge. As the spine moves and the disc is compressed the impurities are squeezed out. Then, as the pressure is released nutrients are drawn in; hence the cleaning process takes place. When the back does not move for long periods of time, movement of the spine is reduced and so, therefore, cleaning and nourishing of the discs are also reduced.

The vertebrae are attached and held together, front and back, by ligaments. Like very strong elastic bands of varying lengths, these ligaments allow certain flexibility and movement of and between the vertebrae. Positioned outside of and along the ligaments are nerves.

The misconception by designers over the past century is partially the belief that the right angle sitting position is accomplished by a 90 degree rotation of the hip joint. Although misinformation about this misconception is supported by most of the design references that are available for use by designers even now, it simply is not possible except on a laboratory skeleton, which can be articulated to assume any position one desires, or a drawing board where designers and human engineers frequently have drawn a standing skeleton from skull to coccyx, with the legs shown arbitrarily rotated 90 degrees and the pelvis shown with no rotation as in the standing position. In actuality such 90 degree rotation of the thigh bone at the hip is prevented by the hamstring muscle and therefore cannot be accomplished by a normal, healthy human being.

What in fact does occur when an individual changes from a standing position to a right angle sitting position is this. First the person bends forward through a rotation of the hip joint. How far one can rotate the hip joint, easily, is controlled by the hamstring muscles, which are attached to the back portion

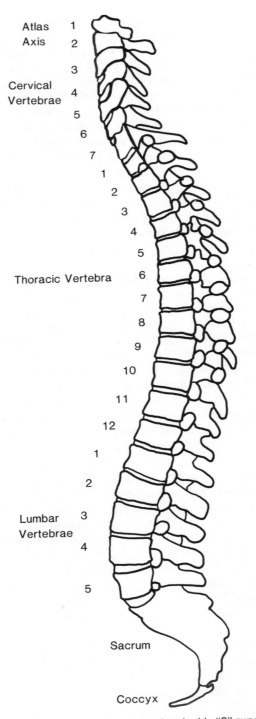

Figure 6.1. Spinal column showing double "S" curve.

of the pelvis, extend along the back of the thigh, and are attached to the lower leg.

As the hip joint is rotated, this muscle becomes increasingly taut until instead of continuing to stretch further, it begins to rotate the pelvis. The actual rotation of the hip joint is approximately 60 degrees. The balance of the 90 degree angle, formed between the torso and the thighs, amounts to about 30 degrees and is accomplished by the rotation of the pelvis.

The lower portion of the spine, specifically the sacrum and the coccyx, are attached to the pelvic ring by tendons in such a manner that when the pelvis is rotated forward or back, the sacrum and coccyx move with it. The effect of this movement, when rotation is forward, is to straighten, or flatten, the lumbar curve.

The individual vertebra is slightly thicker at the front than the back. As long as the spine is in balance, the curve in the lumbar area causes the spaces between the individual vertebrae to remain even without excessive pressure on the intervertebral discs.

When the pelvis is rotated forward, as when moving to the right angle sitting position, the spine is straightened in the lumbar region, forcing the front edges of the lumbar vertebrae closer together and compressing the intervertebral discs. This action is much the same as kids squeezing watermelon seeds between the fingers to make them shoot across the room. Instead of shooting across the room the discs are forced rearward, against the tendons connecting the individual vertebrae.

When pressure on the ligaments is maintained for long periods each day over the years, the ligaments wear, become less able to resist the pressure, and make the individual much more susceptible to a slippage and other disorders of the disc. Whereas an employee with a slipped disc is certainly a productivity loss problem, the majority of time loss because of back ailments is due to much less severe, but still painful conditions.

Pressure on the ligaments caused by compression of the vertebrae also exerts pressure on the nerves that run behind and along the ligaments. The pressure on the nerves will begin to send signals to the brain that all is not well with the lumbar area of the back. The brain signals the body to change position; and so the virtually never-ending, seated back dance begins.

Since no single seated position is comfortable for very long, it is necessary to continually adjust the body for the body to regain a temporary comfortable position.

Reduced to basics, there are only two primary seated positions in the workplace, although each of these will have a number of variations:

1. the work-intensive position and
2. the relaxed, or rest, position.

The work-intensive position is the position used by most people to do work requiring concentration, or work requiring the use of a keyboard, or other equipment. This position is also used when writing or doing other detail work at a worksurface.

The relaxed or rest position is usually assumed by those performing a less intense task such as talking on the telephone or reading. Either position may be found where people are in conferences.

The work-intensive position involves an angle of 90 degrees or less between the torso and the thighs, and the back erect, whereas the relaxed or rest position has an angle of more than 90 degrees between the upper body and the thighs, normally with the chair and the individual's back tilted rearward, away from the worksurface or table.

Now a very important point. It is virtually impossible to maintain the lumbar curve while in the 90 degree, work-intensive position except through the use of sheer muscle force and only for very short periods of time, even then. Further, it is almost impossible to perform most work tasks in this position since it allows no forward bending of the upper torso.

An adjustable lumbar support is both comfortable and healthful when an individual is in the relaxed position; gravity makes it work as the weight of our upper body presses it against the form of the lumbar support. When the same person sits in the work-intensive position the lumbar support is difficult to use and is not needed to maintain a healthy spine.

Children instinctively know to do something to relieve the pressure-on-the-spine situation, although they are not conscious of the fact. How often when we were young were we reprimanded for tilting forward on the front legs of our chairs? Although we did not know it, there was a reason. As we tilted our chairs forward, we increased the angle between our upper torso and our thighs. This act allowed our pelvis to return to its normal standing position, allowed the lumbar portion of our spine to return its normal curve, and removed the pressure from the intervertebral discs in the lumbar region.

Fast forward to now. We are adults and experience the same situation except that now we sit in a chair with a center pedestal. To attempt to tilt the chair forward is risking a nasty fall. What do we do? We slide forward to the front six inches of our chair, which allows us to then drop our knees forward and down and accomplish exactly the same result as we did when we were younger by tilting our chairs forward on the front legs. We increased the 90 degree angle to something approaching 120 degrees, relieving the pressure on the intervertebral discs of our back.

There are many workstation chairs now available in the marketplace and a good many of them are called ergonomic. Ergonomics is biotechnology. Biotechnology has to do with the problems relating to humans using machines: the *human–machine* interface. When a human sits on a chair, any chair, there is, by the very act of sitting, an interface, good, bad, or otherwise. It seems to me that because of that fact alone every chair is an ergonomic chair. Regardless, anyone who spends much time in that chair will have some problems.

There are a few chairs on the market that provide a solution to at least some of the problems of sitting in the workplace, as well as the problems of sitting in other places. There are many more chairs being sold daily that provide little or no appreciable help in alleviating those problems.

Since the greatest problem relative to sitting is caused by the forward rotation of the pelvis as we sit, which has been with us for a very long time, and since physiologically we are not that different from the way we were a hundred years ago, perhaps that is the problem that needs to be addressed first. As I indicated earlier, some European manufacturers, acting on the information in Dr. Mandels writings and those of other researchers, developed workstation seating that addresses the problem of pressure on the intervertebral discs of the lumbar area of the spine.

When we slip to the front six inches of our chairs we gain relief by lowering our knees and increasing the torso/thigh angle. As we solve one problem we create another, however, by reducing the total area on which our buttocks are resting; this soon becomes uncomfortable as well.

One Scandinavian manufacturer, HAG of Norway, developed a seating device that they called the Balans chair; this chair allows users to place their knees, and a portion of their upper body weight on a lower support, while placing the remainder of the weight on the forward sloping seat. Although the Balans chair solves the problem of pressure on the lumbar discs by opening the torso/thigh angle sufficiently, the device cannot be used by all people. Those with knee problems, for instance, who cannot tolerate pressure on their knees, have difficulty using the chair. Since there is no opportunity to adjust the device, the only position available is the work-intensive position. As stated previously, attempting to remain in one position throughout the entire day would be tiring and would therefore decrease productivity.

At least two other European manufacturers developed more conventional workplace chairs. The chairs were fitted, however, with a seat pan that may be adjusted to tilt forward or backward. When the seat is tilted forward the same effect is achieved as when sitting on the front six inches of an ordinary nontilting workstation chair, or when tilting a straight leg chair forward on the front legs. The torso/thigh angle is widened and the disc pressure relieved.

In addition to the lumbar disc problem is the problem of compressing the diaphragm. The diaphragm is the thin membrane that separates the upper and lower portions of our internal organs and is the part with which we breath normally. When our body is bent 90 degrees forward, the function of the diaphragm is impaired. For us to continue breathing the task is taken over by groups of muscles in the neck and shoulder region, a task for which they were never intended, and that after a while may begin to produce tension, stiffness, or pain in the neck and shoulder areas. The blame will usually be directed to something other than the way we are sitting.

The third problem of maintaining a healthy back is the need for spinal movement. The thoracic vertebrae, which are those vertebrae in the area of the rib cage, have very little ability to move because of the ribs. This leaves only the vertebrae of the neck and the lumbar region with much movement capability. Since part of the cleaning and supplying of nutrients to the intervertebral discs relies on movement of the spine, it is important that such movement occur. As a workstation chair is adjusted from the work-intensive to the rest position, some of this movement is supplied. Additional movement, of course, occurs while on break and while away from the workplace.

Since no single position is comfortable for very long, it is important to have a workstation chair that is easily adjustable to accommodate each of the primary positions normally used at the workstation as well as the many variations of each. It is important that adjustment can be easily accomplished or it may be ignored. It is a known fact that as adults we do not always do what is good for us, even though we are aware of the potential consequences of not doing so.

Studies in Europe have shown that when there are too many controls on a workstation chair, too many levers, buttons, knobs, or other adjustment devices, workers will not use them. If the placement or combination of controls is too confusing they will be ignored also. In fact, the studies conclude that if more than two controls are required to be used repeatedly, and if they are not simple to operate, they are likely not to be used at all.

The two most important controls are (1) a gas cylinder-assisted height adjustment, and (2) a single control that allows adjustment of the seat tilt and the forward and backward movement of the back support. Other controls that are adjusted the first time an individual uses a particular chair and only occasionally thereafter are the control that positions the back support vertically, the seat depth if available, and any adjustments for chair arm height or the distance between arms.

Armrests with vertical height adjustment are important, to accommodate the many different size workers. A tall person often will find their arm two to three inches above the armrest on a fixed arm height chair. Short people will discover that their arms must be raised to an unnatural position to place them on the arm rests of the same chair. What happens is that many persons with these measurements ignore the arms altogether and never use them. Workstation chairs with arms that are adjustable solve this problem.

Arm chairs with arms that are simple to adjust vertically work well in multishift situations, where workstations are shared by an individual from each shift. These chairs can quickly and easily be adjusted at each shift change, allowing the same comfort and support for all employees, regardless of their physical size.

Many of the *ergonomic* workstation chairs offered for sale today, some at rather high prices, have controls to rival the space shuttle. If a large amount of money is payed and the controls are seldom if ever used, there is nothing to be gained from the added expenditure. There is certainly no cost effectiveness and the same results for the workers can be accomplished with a much smaller cost. It is important to have workstation chairs that have few controls, and adjustments with the widest ranges, to provide comfort and support the health of the greatest possible number of your employees. The payback will be considerable and ongoing.

FILES AND OTHER STORAGE UNITS

Places to put things is a high priority for most people. Although the need for "hard copy" storage is diminishing, there will always be a need for containers and cabinets in which to store, in an orderly and efficient manner, various records, references, and materials. It is as important now as it has ever been and the types of storage units needed are and will continue to be as various as the items to be stored or filed therein.

Having the right type of storage at the right place and enough of it will make a very important contribution to the goal of increasing white-collar productivity. More and more of what once were considered special storage units are being mass produced by a number of different manufacturers. Storage units should be provided that are intended for the particular type of items you are storing and should be complete with the accessories that make the units simple to use. Again, proper use of the correct storage units will be to your worker's advantage and efficiency, and ultimately to your advantage and increased profit.

ELECTRONIC EQUIPMENT

Each day thee are a number of new electronic devices introduced into the marketplace that are intended to be used in the white-collar workplace. Even more often new models, new variations, and new accessories for the electronic devices already in use by white-collar workers and their management are introduced.

These, and still more like them that are yet to come, constitute the vast array of electronic equipment that must be accommodated by today's workstations and workmodules. Workmodules, of which they become a part, must be flexible enough to accommodate and support the electronic equipment and devices in the workplace.

Some of the more common of these are computers, terminals, monitors, printers, modems, telephones, fax machines, calculators, electronic typewriters, radios, and television. Much of this electronic equipment is very particular as to the power it uses, and the condition of the air in which it operates. The humidity must be within certain limits in either direction and the temperature as well.

Data that go in as well as data that come out must travel over the proper kind of cable with specific types of connectors and in some cases only certain distances to the next device to maintain the proper quality of information. Each of the characteristics for each different piece of electronic equipment may present a challenge to those of you charged with the responsibility for its installation and maintenance. An appropriately designed Beta workplace will give you the flexibility to accommodate the needs of today as well as the needs of the future.

OTHER EQUIPMENT

Other equipment to be used in the white-collar workplace must be electrically operated mechanical or hand-operated mechanical. Electrically operated mechanical equipment includes the electric typewriter, an electric pencil sharpener, or an electric adding machine. A hand-operated mechanical device can be a manual check writer, a paper cutter, or a manual postage meter.

Each of these has one fact in common. Each takes a certain amount of space on the worksurface that must be provided if it is to be used. The electrical devices also have a power requirement that must be taken into account so that the total electrical load for all devices can be adequately provided for. Although the provisions for other equipment may not be as critical and sensitive as some types of electronic equipment, it must be considered and properly accommodated.

7

THE HUMAN ELEMENT: MAN IS THE MEASURE OF ALL THINGS

Man is the measure of all things. This statement made in Italy almost 1500 years ago, is attributed to a Greek philosopher and mathematician, Pythagorus of Samos.

It was the belief of Pythagorus and his followers that the proper measurements for all things could be determined by using the same relative proportions as those found on the human body.

Some consider this an exaggeration and others consider it nonsense. Whatever we may believe about the statement as originally used, it contains a great truth.

Because if individuals are to work efficiently in the workplaces of today and tomorrow, then the measurements of those individuals, male and female, fat and thin, short and tall, young and old, must be considered and accommodated.

Let us paraphrase Pythagorus of Samos and say that *Man, or Woman, is the Measure of All Things, which either is to use efficiently.*

In his book *Office Hazards—How Your Job Can Make You Sick*, Joel Makower writes concerning the problem:

> The frustrations inherent in the "one-size-fits-all" approach to office furniture design are best demonstrated in a classic 1952 study performed by G.S. Daniels for the United States Air Force.
>
> Daniels was charged with the mission of determining how many Air Force pilots would be considered "average" in terms of ten body measurements designed into Air Force clothing. He studied the measurements of 4,063 Air Force flyers to see how they compared with the "average" clothing they were wearing. He didn't even use an exact figure; in order to qualify as "average" an individual's measurements only had to be within 15 percent above or below the actual average measurement—a range of 30 percent. Here's what Daniels found:
>
> - Of 4,063 men, 1,055 were of "average" height.
> - Of those 1,055 men, 302 were also of "average" chest circumference.

- Of those 302 men, 143 were also of "average" sleeve length.
- Of those 143 men, 73 were also of "average" crotch circumference.
- Of those 73 men, 28 were also of "average" torso circumference.
- Of those 28 men, 12 were also of "average" hip circumference.
- Of those 12 men, 6 were also of "average" neck circumference.
- Of those 6 men, 3 were also of "average" waist circumference.
- Of those 3 men, 2 were also of "average" thigh circumference.
- Of those two men, none was also of "average" crotch length.

So much for "average" people. But that hasn't stopped furniture manufacturers from designing products for the "average" office worker.*

Panero and Zelnick in *Human Dimension and Interior Space* state that

a very serious error in the application of data is to assume that the 50th percentile dimensions represent the measurements of an "average man" and to create a design to accommodate 50th percentile data.

Dr. H. T. E. Hertzberg, a distinguished physical research anthropologist, indicated in an article for *Contract* magazine that the so-called average man is a myth. He says,

There is really no such thing as an "average" man or woman. There are men who are average in weight, or in stature, or in sitting height, but the men who are average in two dimensions constitute only about 7 percent of the population; those in three, only about 3 percent; those in four, less than 2 percent. There are no men average in as few as 10 dimensions. Therefore the concept of the "average" man is fundamentally incorrect, because no such creature exists. Workplaces to be efficient should be designed according to the measured range of body size.†

Although there is no *average man* or *average woman* to accommodate, there is a vast workforce of individuals whose various dimensional extremes are known and need to be accommodated.

Not so long ago the ability to adjust the dimensions of office furniture was at best very limited, if it existed at all. Then as the situation improved, adjustments still could satisfy only portions of the working population because the ranges of adjustment were insufficient. Controls were often difficult to reach, or difficult to operate, or both. Even small improvements in the ability to adjust, and the range of those adjustments, was a welcome occurrence.

The problem can be attributed to a number of factors. First, it can be attributed to a lack of knowledge on the manufacturer's part as to the need and to their reluctance to make available features that will, at best, result in a

---

*Excerpted with permission.
†Reproduced with permission of *Contract* magazine from the September 1970 issue.

relatively small number of sales. Second, the problem can be attributed to an attitude by many business owners and managers that whatever office workers are given, in the way of furniture and equipment, is all that is needed; that individuals should *make do with whatever they are given.* Contributing, further, to the problem is a widespread lack of knowledge on the part of owners and managers as to what such an attitude is costing them in terms of lost productivity, and consequently lost profit dollars as well. The same owners and managers are frequently unaware of what is available to solve the problem should they have the desire to do so.

It has been said that manufacturers had a long way to go to solve most of the problems created by office furniture that is not conducive to white-collar productivity improvement; not so long ago that was true. The truth, now, is that many such manufacturers have only a short way to travel. Given a lack of desire or adequate incentive, it can be a very long distance.

It is extremely important to remember two facts when creating anything for use in the environment of the white-collar workplace. The wheel does not have to be reinvented. Keeping what is good and improving what needs to be improved make good business sense. Unfortunately, what frequently happens is that good functional design is sacrificed in the name of something new; which may be pleasing to look at, but which is lacking in ability to improve or even maintain the same level of productivity as what it replaces. New, somehow, is often mistakenly perceived as better, simply because it is new. As previously stated, function and beauty are not mutually exclusive. They can, and must, coexist if the workplace is to be optimized.

DESIGN CRITERIA

The design criteria for optimizing the workplace can be found in a number of references. These are found in the selected bibliography and are preceded by an asterisk.

In these and other books, manufacturers, for example, will find the information that is necessary to make products functionally efficient. Attractiveness is subjective, however, and what is attractive to some may be abhorent to other potential customers. Also, the office furniture business is not one that lends itself to built-in obsolescense; office furniture in particular seems to go on forever. Fads on the other hand are an entirely different thing.

MANAGEMENT CONTRIBUTION

Although everyone wins with a Beta workplace, the organization itself has the greatest potential for gain. The majority of businesses exist for the primary purpose of making money, and that is precisely what the Beta workplace can produce for any company that will invest in the methods and techniques of the

Beta workplace solution in order to experience the rewards that are inherent therein. Management's first contribution is the decision to grab the opportunity to increase productivity in their white-collar operation.

The second, and just as important, contribution to be made by management at all levels is to give the program your complete and wholehearted support. There may be a selling job to sceptics within the management ranks. Support and selling are needed at all levels of managements. A solid, unified effort will provide rewards for everyone and a successful climb for the organization.

It is important for management to understand the basic concept behind the Beta solution—what it is that makes it work when other solutions fail. The most important fact of the program is that the individual is the key. The individual is important to the point that it is the individual who can make any productivity effort succeed or fail. A single individual may not be able to bring down an entire program, but that individual can certainly stop or reduce the success of their part of that program. But that is negative thinking. On the positive side, various studies have shown that most workers want to work; most want to do a good job. The opportunity for management is to provide the opportunity for those workers to succeed, and the corporation with them. The Beta sector program described herein is the vehicle of opportunity for that success.

The reason that the Beta program can succeed is that it takes into account the strengths and weaknesses of all workers as human beings. The program then utilizes each person's strengths and compensates for their weaknesses to make the entire work process a more pleasant and rewarding experience. The program further acknowledges even minor variations in the job descriptions of each worker and makes certain that those variations are provided for in the workstations and workmodules that are provided for the conduct of the work tasks required of that position.

When it is easier to work, people who already want to work will do so, and do so more efficiently. As I said previously, this program is not a panacea, and will not solve all management problems in the workplace. The Beta program will not cause a person who does not want to work to do so, very often. It will not cause an individual who cannot write a letter to suddenly be able to compose impressive business letters, or even acceptable ones. It will provide the optimum setting for workers to perform to the level that they are naturally, through education and by training, capable.

Last, but in many instances the most important aspect of the Beta program, is that it involves each of the workers in the design process. Each individual has the opportunity to provide input. That fact is important to the worker and it is important to the organization.

Management's contribution through its participation and support, at all levels, is essential to a successful productivity improvement program. The message to be delivered is that the entire organization is involved in something to make work life better for everyone in the workplace.

WHO'S RUNNING THE BUSINESS?

Many times executives and managers have asked for the solution to a particular problem. Then, on hearing the consultant's recommended solution, the manager or executive responds, *We can't do that, Betty Secretary would really be upset*; or *John Supervisor wouldn't go along with that*; and even, *Elizabeth Manager might quit if we were to do what you suggest.*

Anytime such dialogue takes place it is immediately obvious that the problem being discussed is minor by comparison to a much larger problem that clearly exists and that is probably robbing the organization of some of its productivity. The much larger problem is identified by the question, *Who is running the business, management or the employees?*

It is extremely important that all workers have input into the what, why, and how of the workplace, with its workstations and workmodules, and other special equipment. Generally, however, employees who should not be making the decisions, are causing decisions, to be made as to what the specifics are to be. More important, those individuals should not be allowed to coerce or blackmail management into accepting their wishes. In such instances the act of coercion indicates a lack of cooperation on the part of an individual; an attitude problem. Further the correct solution must be evenly applied for the ultimate good of the organization and all employees, and, therefore, should respond to the needs and requirements of the job description of each individual worker, independent of all other workers.

It is easy to overlook relatively minor variations in the task requirements of one worker as compared to the tasks of another worker with the same job designation and the seemingly identical job description. It is true that such variations should be known and understood by that individual's supervisor. For a number of reasons, however, the supervisor may not be aware of the need, and it goes unnoticed, is not provided for, and becomes a weak link in the quest for increased profit.

There are many consultants in the field who suggest surveying only samples of each type of worker, or each type of job designation. There are costs that accrue to the consultant as a result of conducting the very important individual survey. If this survey is eliminated fees can be reduced, or additional profit for the consultant can be made. In my opinion, eliminating the every person survey can result in questionable, if not inaccurate, results being obtained. Again, an equally important objective of the survey of each individual's needs is the inclusion of their input into the design process, and the resulting interest and cooperation that normally result.

When the above information has been obtained and analyzed, the designers and management can use it to formulate the plan, and will have the data supporting the decisions that must be made to implement the opportunities for increased productivity and profit. Then there will be no question as to what is required in the workplace and there will be no question as to who is running the business.

8

THE PREMIUM
AND THE COST

Virtually any item, whether it is a piece of equipment, a workmodule, a system of any kind, even an entire environment, if it is cost effective, will likely have a cost premium over items of a similar nature that are not cost effective or that are less cost effective. It will almost invariably cost more to obtain the cost benefits available and the return on investment desired.

Some owners and managers view business as a game. Others see their business as one gamble after another. But whether you see your operation as a gamble, a game, or neither, the facts are simple. In most instances when it relates to cost effectiveness you have to pay to play. There is always the choice not to play. If you choose not to play, it is true that there is no chance that you will lose anything. If you choose not to play there is also no opportunity to benefit or to win.

Why is it that individuals who would never consider risking anything where they believe there is a possibility that they might lose all or part of what is at risk will gamble virtually everything they possess if they are convinced that there is no risk, that their venture or investment is a sure thing? This kind of tendency on the part of otherwise conservative and prudent businessmen and others has led to the utterance of the warning—*If it seems too good to be true, it probably is.*

Much has been promised in the interest of productivity improvement, particularly in the white-collar area. In some instances much has been delivered; in other cases nothing has been delivered; and in still other situations virtually every percentage point in between much and nothing appears to have been delivered, some high, many more low or very low. This kind of track record has resulted in the cultivation of a high level of skepticism among business owners and managers regarding anyone's ability to deliver predictable increases in the productivity of their employees.

Results have frequently been disappointing as various management teams have attempted to increase individual white-collar productivity. One factor

67

that contributes to this kind of result is that often individual workers are largely ignored except during periods where an effort was being made to change them, or an attempt made to cause them to try to change themselves. Although there is nothing wrong with successes that have been realized, another fertile field, in the Beta Sector, has been waiting to be discovered.

As indicated in earlier chapters success in the Beta Sector of white-collar productivity can range from 10 to 30 percent, or more. These gains are available without having to change the individual workers. To accomplish these increases, however, certain changes in your workplace are required. In most instances that will require capital expenditures of one kind or another, and usually more than one kind.

If you are moving into a new workplace all that is required is that you observe the requirements regarding systems furniture and other furniture, and select the required kinds of finish materials. That is really all that is necessary to create an optimized workplace that will allow your workers to deliver the productivity of which they are capable, willingly. There may be premiums to pay for the finish materials. This depends on what you would use ordinarily. If you normally would seek the absolutely least cost to put you into your company's new home, then there will be premiums to pay. For those with this philosophy regarding the furnishing of their workplace there will be no payback, only a pay out. If the materials you would normally choose are the materials that do the job best, whatever the cost, there may be little or no premium. The materials recommended and the systems furniture we propose are not the most expensive of what is available. Most of the products fall into medium or slightly above price ranges.

With the Beta Solution your money can come flowing back to you and then add to your bottom line over the years. It is like successful weight reduction or gain. First there is the necessity to change your mindset relative to what will accomplish your goal. Once the goal is achieved, you must change your fiscal life-style to maintain it.

This chapter is about the premiums your firm must pay to achieve the goal of increased productivity by your white-collar workforce. It is also about the new life-style that will not only return your investment in a short period of time, but will continue to provide a return in the form of increased profit in the years following.

PRODUCTS AND MATERIALS

We list in this chapter eight materials or types of items that are essential to creating the Beta workplace. These are (1) three-ring binders, (2) carpet, (3) wall covering, (4) window treatment methods and materials, (5) ceilings, (6) light fixtures, (7) electronic sound masking, and (8) workmodules.

Three-Ring Binders

Since there is usually a gasp of disbelief on the mention of three-ring binders as a contributor to productivity improvement, I will address this item first. The binders themselves are not the problem, but the most frequent color used is. That color is black and these items are turned out annually by the thousands and contribute not only to such things as fatigue factors but also to increased energy costs. How can that be?

There are organizations that have entire walls of black three-ring binders and the reflectivity of the color black is 0. Most of the light that contacts the black surface of the binders is absorbed rather than reflected for more efficient use of energy. To attain the same visual comfort level in that area it is necessary to increase the amount of ambient light, at additional energy cost. The same binders in any of a number of lighter colors will contain the material therein just as well and brighten up the space at the same time.

When black binders are used in workstation shelves above the worksurface a fatigue factor comes with them. As the worker's eyes are lifted from the light colored work material on the worksurface to the black binders, the irises of their eyes will open wide to allow more light to enter. Then as the worker looks again to the work material on the worksurface, the irises contract. Over the course of the work period, depending on the tasks that are being performed, this process will be repeated many times, contributing to the overall fatigue level for the worker. This fatigue factor associated with the binders can be eliminated by using binders that are light in color. Lighter colored binders are generally more expensive. If you buy in large quantities the difference will not be so great, but there may be a premium. As I have pointed out previously, there is also a quick payback and the binders become part of the solution, not part of the problem on the road to increased profit.

Carpet

There are basically five types of carpet that are used for workplace interiors as discussed in this book. These are (1) modular carpet (also referred to as carpet tiles or carpet squares), which is free-layed except for an adhesive grid, (2) narrow roll carpet with a resilient backing, (3) broadloom carpet glued directly to the floor, (4) broadloom carpet stretched over a pad, and (5) area rugs such as oriental carpets. The carpets are listed in the order of desirability and performance as relates to productivity improvement and flexibility, and cost effectiveness. Flexibility, ease of handling, and installation are major benefits of the first two only, however.

Any carpet will contribute the primary functions of floor covering. These are sound absorption, impact noise deadening, and fatigue reduction. Carpet becomes a premium finish only when it is used instead of various types of resilient floor coverings such as vinyl sheet goods, vinyl tile, and rubber sheet goods or squares. Carpet will often actually be less expensive than hard surface flooring such as hardwood planks or parquet tile or quarry tile, and other types of ceramic tile. In such cases the carpet is not only a premium, it actually results in a savings.

Modular carpet may also be considered premium when because of its qualities of flexibility, longer life potential, and/or its required use with flat power, phone, and data wire and cable it is selected over lower end broadloom carpet.

Wall Covering

Wall covering recommended for use on core walls, columns, and other vertical surfaces has a premium due to its sound-attenuating characteristics (as explained in Chapter 4). The ability of walls and other vertical surfaces to intercept sound and to weaken or remove it from the workplace, rather than reflect it to another ear or surface, is extremely important to removing aural distraction.

Sound-attenuating wall covering makes a necessary and desirable contribution to the maximization of the workplace. Its cost premium depends on the reference material. When this sound-absorbing material is compared to paint, for instance, it has a premium. When compared to various wall treatments available, the cost can range from premium, to trade-off, to savings, depending on the cost of the specific wall covering with which it is being compared.

Window Treatment Methods and Materials

Window treatments such as horizontal or vertical louvers, shades, or draperies are normally used for solar control and for privacy, in most workplaces. Window treatments also are a necessary component of a workplace that is conducive to maximum output by white-collar workers, and may or may not carry a premium cost. If the same type of window treatment would be used for solar protection, privacy, or aesthetic reasons, then there is no premium to the cost. If a different window treatment would likely be used, either because of its preferred appearance or because of its lower price, then certainly the recommended treatment carries with it a cost premium. The recommended treatment also provides the benefit of cost effectiveness.

Ceilings

The ceiling will always have a cost premium unless something other than a commodity type ceiling has been specified or selected. Ceilings are manufactured and installed by the millions of square feet to meet minimum building code requirements for fire protection and to provide a place to install minimal fluorescent ambient light fixtures, and the minimum number of supplies and returns for the heating, ventilating, and air conditioning system.

There are exceptions, of course, and in situations where ceilings have been selected for acoustical performance, fire protection, and appearance, there is a very good chance that no additional premium will be necessary because of what has already been specified.

Light Fixtures

Good lighting, adequate lighting, efficient lighting, and appropriate lighting, as we have previously discussed, are extremely important to each of us. More lighting is not necessarily better lighting. In some instances less is not only better, but is essential. The right amount of lighting will provide the correct illumination throughout the workplace based solely on the tasks that are to be performed there, taking into account all other aspects of good lighting. There are any number of special purpose areas that require specific lighting such as CADD or other types of computer input areas. I have mentioned the desirability of having an acoustical consultant on your project. Equally important is having a lighting consultant. A lighting consultant should normally be different from your electrical engineer. The lighting consultant will design the lighting to provide the appropriate lighting for your particular workplace. Like everything else about the Beta program, the fees that you will pay will be returned to you as a result of your program. The lighting program is cost effective also. Energy conservation is part of that program.

Electronic Sound Masking

The only premium for electronic sound masking is reflected in the cost difference between a system that is effective and produces the desired results and a system that promises much masking for little cost and that contributes more to the problem than the solution, or a system that promises much masking for considerable cost but does not solve the problem or, the difference between having an effective electronic masking system and no masking system at all. From these perspectives there is no premium, since the recommended system is the only one that produces the solution being sought.

Workmodules

Here we enter the world of overchoice, partial solutions, and trade-offs. There is, in my opinion, no perfect systems furniture and no perfect furniture. All have features that are desirable, and all are lacking in some way or other. A few manufacturers have devised features that are somewhat unique, and they will be watched by the competition for acceptance by end users. If the features are accepted, at least some of the competition will then copy it into their own systems.

The truth is that most systems are enough alike that to the people who buy them, they are the same. Systems furniture is both necessary and desirable to optimize the white-collar workplace. When comparison is made to desks and chairs, based on cost alone there is a rather sizable premium. Systems furniture can deliver operating cost savings, however, which translates to your bottom line. Desks and chairs, used in conventional ways, cannot. The premium that you must pay to have systems furniture rather than desks and chairs is the bad news. The good news is that you can get your money back and then realize added profit because of your investment in systems furniture.

9

THE BENEFITS

Prudent businessmen and managers the world over will ask when considering something new for which they are contemplating an expenditure, "What is the cost? What is the benefit? Is it cost effective?" Frequently the answer to these questions determines what the decision will be. There are benefits enough for everyone when productivity improvement is accomplished through the methods and techniques described herein. The benefits after all are the incentives that encourage all employees to participate and provide the cooperation necessary for any successful productivity improvement program.

INFORMATION WORKERS

A large number of benefits accrue to the individual workers. Chief among these benefits is the opportunity to perform their work, which at times may be boring and repetitious, in an optimum workstation located in an optimum workplace. Such a work environment allows the individual to perform his or her work with very little, or no inadvertent distraction and with relatively minimal physical and mental effort for the type of work each is performing, particularly when compared to the same work being performed in a more conventional workplace.

The techniques described herein are formulated to humanize the workspace as much as possible and, when followed completely, will provide a pleasant working environment. All of these benefits contribute to a feeling of well being, a state that virtually all of us seek, and certainly a benefit that, for most of us, is worth working for. We all know how much better our performance is at any task or activity when we are feeling positive. Or the difference when we are well physically with no nagging aches or pains as opposed to when the pain is there. We also know how devastating it can be to face financial and emotional

73

problems, when we have no obvious solution or remedy. It is easy to believe that each of us is the only person so burdened, and when we do feel that way, every small problem becomes magnified.

Consider that any worker may have one of the above conditions affecting their life at a particular time, or maybe two of the above, or three, plus some we do not even imagine. Perhaps because they are a conscientious, loyal employee, or maybe because of a temporary financial squeeze they feel they could not afford to miss the work, or it could be that they know their input is needed because their team is in a critical phase of a project. Whatever the reason, and regardless of the personal problems the workers are dealing with, they still have reported for work. It does not take a psychologist to know that even with the good intentions, the productivity will suffer.

If, in addition to the above mentioned internal distractions the workers have, they must also deal with the many distractions of most workplaces, it is easy to see how the productivity loss potential can continue to grow. The Beta workplace can help to minimize the problems each worker brings to the workplace. Since there is no known way to prevent the personal problems we all have, minimizing their effect is the next best thing.

Although this book deals only superficially with the aesthetic aspects of the workplace, such visual treatment is extremely important. The ambiance of the workplace does affect the way workers feel about the organization for which they work and about themselves. Such feelings then affect the way the workers perform and in may cases even the way they dress. Workers who before came to the workplace in casual attire, or jeans, are seen to begin wearing more business-like attire. It is important that workers feel good as much as possible—feel good about the work they do and feel good about the organization they work for. This is, or should be, the primary effect sought for the individual worker, in any productivity improvement effort.

SUPERVISORS

Supervisors benefit from anything that causes their workers to perform their work more willingly, more accurately, and over a smaller period of time. When such a condition exists it allows the supervisor to concentrate on ways to improve the operation in their area of responsibility, rather than having to continually arbitrate minor differences and personal complaints. Supervisors often will find a greater degree of involvement and cooperation from those whose work they direct. Each supervisor also receives the benefits enjoyed by those whom they supervise.

MANAGERS

Managers, like supervisors, gain not only from the advantages of an optimum workplace environment in which to perform their own managerial tasks, but will also find it easier to commit for and deliver greater output. For managers, the opportunity can then exist for the introduction of creative new ideas. New approaches can be tried and developed in an atmosphere of cooperation and higher morale. One of the jobs of managers is to reduce the cost of operation. Most managers, at one time or another, have been responsible for finding a means to cause a sizable increase in the productivity of the people assigned to their profit center. Rehashing the old ideas has led only to frustration and a disappointing annual review, at best. At the worst, managers have found themselves mailing out resumes and wondering if there actually is a solution to the seemingly never ending problem of greater output and greater profit. One answer is here.

EXECUTIVES, OWNERS, AND STOCKHOLDERS

Executives and owners are usually the ones who have to agree to pay-to-play. The cost to implement the application of techniques and methods proposed and described in this book is no different from other expenditures, for capital improvements. An investment must be made, or a premium paid. There is a difference from many white-collar productivity solutions, however, and that is the fact that this solution is cost effective, when used properly.

The potential for reducing the cost of operation and increasing the opportunity for additional profit is very real and obtainable. The payback period is short, and the reward of increased and continuing operational cost savings is limited only by the size of your organization.

10

WORKPLACE FLEXIBILITY

For management to be able to respond efficiently to the need for physical change in support of organizational realignment, the facility must have an integral element of flexibility. The majority of businesses have their white-collar workplaces put together as if there was never to be a change of any kind in the organization. Others who strive for flexibility do not think the problem all the way through, or have consultants who do not understand the problem, or who do not know the solutions.

Not so long ago, it was quite normal for a business to be located in a space with the same offices and bull pens from the day the doors were opened until the business was closed many years later. During the period that the business was in operation, virtually nothing in the physical plant changed. The walls, the doors, the offices, the bull pens all remained in the same location as business was conducted within those fixed barriers.

If any changes were made, it was the people who were moved to accommodate the building. In many instances where physical change of the workspace was clearly indicated, it was postponed and the spaces were expected to be used *as is*, with management considering the inconveniences and the reduced productivity an acceptable trade-off.

As technology progresses and as reduced productivity is less and less an acceptable option, new methods are available that allow management to respond to the need for physical change with a minimum of disruption and distraction in the workspace. The elements of the workplace interior that allow this response consist of the following.

ELECTRONIC MASKING SYSTEM

The electronic masking system (EMS) is a very important element and contributes considerably to flexibility in that it allows virtually infinite opportunity to reconfigure the workplace without sacrificing either freedom from distraction or confidentiality. Once installed, the EMS can be almost ignored when changes are made, except for conference areas, some private offices, and some special purpose areas.

The most often used construction for interior partitions is 2 inch by 4 inch (51 by 102 mm) steel studs located at 16 inches (406 mm), center-to-center, and covered with ½ inch or ⅝ inch (12.7 mm or 15.9 mm) plasterboard on each side. The interior spaces between the studs may or may not be filled with sound-absorbing material to reduce the amount of sound passing from one side of the wall to the other, and to maintain confidentiality for the words spoken in the space that is enclosed by the partition.

The partition may be constructed to the underside of the ceiling or it may be continued on up to the structure of the roof or the floor above. If the partition reaches only the ceiling, some type of acoustical barrier must close off the space between the ceiling and the floor or roof construction above. The same type of sound barrier is used to stop sound passage above movable or demountable partitions that extend only from the floor to the ceiling.

A sound barrier will likely be made of sheet lead, while a curtain or blanket will be of a loose fiber material such as fiberglass or rock wool, often with a very thin metal face on one or both surfaces. Both of these materials, while somewhat effective when properly installed, often have sound leaks that occur when the curtains are fit around steel joists, pipe, air ducts, electrical conduit, and various types of equipment with which it shares the ceiling plenum.

A difficulty to be dealt with, however, occurs when the partition over which the barrier or blanket is located is moved. Frequently the sound barriers or blankets are forgotten or overlooked altogether. If not forgotten, trying to move the blankets or barriers is an extremely difficult and frustrating task. The materials normally are easy to damage and it is frequently less expensive to purchase and install new barriers or blankets than to relocate existing ones.

Electronic sound masking gives you all of the benefits of barriers and blankets and more, and requires no changes when partitions are moved except for some tuning of individual sound masking generators or speakers. If you presently have an installation that uses barriers or blankets and you want to be confident that your conversations are not leaking to unwanted ears, EMS, properly installed, will plug those leaks permanently.

THE FLEXIBLE CEILING

A flexible ceiling means simply that the ceiling and certain of the elements that are mounted to it, in it, and on it, may be readily and easily rearranged or moved within certain ranges of location in order to accommodate reconfigured workspaces below it, without the disruption and dirt of major construction. The ceiling when properly designed and specified will provide a visible grid that serves both as a ready guide for space planning as well as a convenient reference for a building and site locator, an important part of inventory maintenance.

It is a good idea to base the dimensions of the ceiling suspension system, or grid, on the building module, if at all possible. The grid should accommodate the simple attachment of removable anchors for full height movable partitions without being easily damaged. The ceiling grid should have a flat or satin finish to provide minimal brightness on the ceiling. Any time workers look at the ceiling they need to see a consistent and nonbright surface. Even the correct light fixtures are only slightly brighter than the surrounding ceiling and grid.

When a worker looks up at the ceiling and sees brightness, whether it is caused by strong light reflecting off of the ceiling board or grid or by brightness on the surface of a flat lensed light fixture, an after-image in the shape of the bright area or areas is formed in the eye of the worker. When workers return their eyes again to the material on which they are working, the after-image will appear to be suspended between them and the work material, or superimposed on the work material, obscuring the worker's view of that material. In a few moments the after-image will fade away and viewing by the worker will return to normal. During this period, however, that individual's productivity will be lessened. Over the course of an entire work day this action will occur a number of times. Measured on an annual basis this distraction will amount to a substantial number.

Ceiling Board

The ceiling board is an extremely important part of the entire acoustical treatment package, and needs to be selected in consideration of a number of performance criteria as follows.

Fire Rating. If your building has a fire protection rating independent of the ceiling, then the fire rating of the ceiling board may not be a consideration. It is important that you know what the situation is because your ceiling must satisfy the local building and fire protection codes before you will be issued an occupancy permit. If your particular building needs a fire-rated ceiling to meet code requirements, then your options will be more limited as to which ceiling boards may be selected for use in your workspaces.

Acoustical Characteristics. How well a ceiling board performs acoustically determines how much of a contribution that particular ceiling will make toward reducing sensory distraction caused by airborne sounds that enter the workplace. It is important to determine how much of the sound that contacts the ceiling board will be reflected back into the workspace, how much will be absorbed by the board, and how much sound will pass through the board into the space above the ceiling, contact the floor or roof structure, and reflect back into the workplace at another location.

Reflectivity. Ceiling board should reflect the majority of the light that comes in contact with it. When it is necessary to trade-off between acoustical properties and reflectivity, acoustical properties should be given priority, but only to a point. Ceiling material should have a reflectance in excess of 70 percent. There is a difference between the reflectivity we are seeking and the brightness we want to prevent.

Flexibility. In this case flexibility depends on accessibility. It is extremely desirable and necessary to be able to access many of the pieces of equipment, pipes, controls, and so on that are located in the ceiling plenum. It is necessary to be able to easily relocate light fixtures to different locations in the ceilings during reconfiguration of the workspace below it. Properly designed and installed, the fixtures can be relocated without being disconnected, a saving in itself. More important is the fact that you have control over the light levels in the workplace. Having appropriate light levels at workstations removes certain fatigue factors and increases productivity.

Conditioned Air. Conditioned air is normally introduced into or removed from the workspace through grilles or louvers located in the ceiling. Air boots that connect flexible ducts to the louvers or grilles must be capable of being easily relocated to allow reconfiguration of enclosed spaces with minimal difficulty and without restricting conditioned air distribution or air return. Air boots on flexible duct must have appropriate provisions for fire dampers located at the louver, as required by codes and as are necessary. These fire dampers close automatically in case of a fire, preventing smoke from circulating though the workplace or to other parts of the building by way of the duct system.

LIGHT: ARTIFICIAL AND NATURAL

Light, whether in the form of natural light coming through the workplace windows or skylights, or light artificially created with ambient, task, and decorative light fixtures, costs money to create or to control, or both. When light comes into contact with any surface, some of the light will be absorbed by the material, and the balance will be reflected back into the space from which it came. The lighter the color, the more of the light that contacts the colored surface will be reflected, not absorbed. The more light that is reflected from one surface to another, and then on to still another, the less energy is necessary to provide the required illumination for that part of the workspace.

Ambient Light Fixtures

To provide flexibility, light fixtures must provide a distribution pattern that is similar in all directions, provide low brightness at the ceiling surface, and not provide a reflecting surface for airborne sound. Workstation and workmodule layouts and configurations should not have to be constantly referenced to light fixture orientation to produce quality light at sufficient levels for the tasks being performed. The fixture must be easily cleaned and relamped and, ideally, the ballast easily replaced.

To obtain the above features generally requires the following. The light fixture will be a 2 × 2 (610 mm by 610 mm) foot lay-in type fixture. It will likely have two 40 watt "U"-shaped fluorescent tubes, and will have a parabolic reflector or a parabolic louver. The fixture will be easy to relamp and clean, and have a modular ballast to facilitate ballast replacement when necessary. Ballasts also will be adjustable. This adjustability allows additional energy savings by taking advantage of favorable reflectivity of workplace materials when the fluorescent lamps are new. As the lamps age and their output is reduced, the ballasts can be adjusted to extend the life of the lamp and maintain the necessary illumination throughout the life of the lamp.

Task Light Fixtures

Task light fixtures, as the name suggests, are fixtures that are not used to provide overall lighting of the workplace or workstation. These fixtures fall into basically two categories. The first is a fixed fluorescent tube variety, with one or two 15-watt to 30-watt lamps, which may have a diffuser or not, and may have a slight degree of adjustability by way of tilting the entire fixture or moving the fixture laterally toward or away from the worker. This type of task light fixture is used primarily to erase shadows caused by shelves of system furniture workmodules.

The second type of task light fixture is designed to furnish a worker with a great deal of adjustability. This allows workers to place light where they need it while performing the particular task at hand. Later the fixture may be adjusted to concentrate light in an altogether different area of the worksurface. Task lights such as these furnish the opportunity to provide a wide range of illumination to accommodate variations in light level required for different workers because of age and/or work materials.

Special functions require special parameters relating to task lighting. In areas where computer aided design and drafting (CADD) tasks, or desktop publishing, or other computer graphics tasks are being performed, there is a requirement for reduced ambient light levels, but there is also the need to read reference materials. The lower ambient light level is easy enough to accomplish. There is a need for a task light that gives some adjustability for light level, sufficient light on the reference material, and virtually no light, less than 0.5 footcandle (fc) in some instances, hitting the monitor tube face. These parameters are necessary to prevent reflections on the face of the monitor tube that cause reduced contrast between the information on the screen and the screen background. Such lack of contrast makes it more difficult for the worker to read the information on the screen and contributes to worker fatigue. This is a fatigue factor that can and should be reduced or removed.

Decorative Light Fixtures

Decorative light fixtures, although they contribute to the overall light level, generally are not required as either ambient or task lighting per se. Decorative lighting, as its designation implies, is primarily for aesthetic purposes and may be as diverse as wall and floor lamps, wall sconces, some types of hanging fixture, and chandeliers. It may also be a decorative neon sign or other illuminated decorative piece.

Lighting Controls

Another feature that is part of the overall lighting system includes sensors that determine the amount of artificial light required by monitoring the amount of natural light entering the workspace through the windows or atriums and that control the level at which the ambient light fixtures operate. The amount of energy used by the light fixtures is reduced because the fixture produces only the amount of additional light needed; this is a real energy saver.

PARTITIONS: FLOOR TO CEILING

Interior partitions fall generally into three types: (1) fixed, (2) demountable, and (3) movable.

In many workplaces there will be a need for two types of floor to ceiling partitions, in addition to the systems furniture of the open plan. Fixed or demountable partitions are used in the area for corporate executive officers for functional reasons: the need for a high level of confidentiality and a need for isolation for concentration. In addition, there is often the need for informal conferences, and in some cases formal conferences, to be held in the executive's personal office.

Movable partitions are used for executives and for upper level managers who are located with their units in or adjacent to open plan systems furniture areas. Movable partitions provide the flexibility needed for workplace reconfiguration, when it is required. Movable partitions, while providing attractive floor to ceiling division of the space, also allow the freedom to use all areas of your workplace except for core areas, which are permanently fixed.

Fixed Partitions

Full height (to the ceiling or structure) fixed partitions are in a sense like fences. They are put there to keep things, including people, out. The reason may be for purposes of privacy for confidentiality or privacy for concentration. Each is valid and necessary for certain individuals for specific reasons. The job description if correctly written and descriptive of the tasks required will indicate the necessity for privacy, or lack thereof.

Fixed partitions are most often made of steel or sometimes wood studs, over which is placed plasterboard. The studs fit into and are screwed to steel floor and ceiling channels if they are steel, and are nailed to a wood base plate and header if they are wood. The base plate or channel and the header or ceiling channel are fastened securely to the floor and ceiling, respectively. The plasterboard is attached to the steel studs with special screws and to the wood studs with special nails or screws. The joints between the sheets of plasterboard are then covered with joint tape, which is made of paper, covered with joint compound, smoothed and sanded. The screw or nail heads are similarly covered with joint compound and sanded. The partition is then ready for paint or, after receiving a coat of sizing, is ready for various types of wallpaper or wall covering. When completed, this wall is fixed.

To relocate this type of partition it is normally demolished and thrown away. Then a new wall of the same type is constructed in a new location. Construction or demolition of fixed partitions is a relatively noisy operation and produces construction debris, dust, and grit, particularly during sanding operations. If work is being done in areas occupied by white-collar workers, distraction will vary but can be considerable, depending on the construction crew.

If at all possible the construction area should be temporarily partitioned off and sealed. Special attention needs to be given to the problems of dust and grit produced and the exposure of electronic devices to those contaminants. More of this type of work is being done on evenings and weekends, when the office workers are away from the workplace. Sealing off the area is desirable and cost effective, even though the white collar-workers are not in the workspace.

Demountable Partitions

Demountable partitions are usually constructed of steel studs that fit into steel floor and ceiling channels or runners. These are in turn securely attached to the floor and ceiling by various methods. The floor channels are frequently, although not always, anchored to the floor with powder driven fasteners and to the ceiling grid with special screws. The steel studs may snap or clip into the ceiling and floor channels. Panels may be of steel, and be vinyl wrapped or enameled. Panels may also be plasterboard, plain, steel clad and enameled, or vinyl wrapped. Variations of the above panels, including wood, are also available. Different methods are used to attach or secure the panels to the stud framework. Bases may be enameled metal or vinyl. Doors have steel frames and are usually enameled steel, prefinished wood veneer, or plastic laminate.

Demountable partitions may be disassembled and reassembled at a new location. With steel panels, the partitions may be 90 percent or more reusable. If the panels are plasterboard the factor for reuse drops considerably.

Installation as well as take-down and relocation are relatively noisy and produce construction debris in various amounts. If work is being done in areas occupied by white-collar workers, the distraction will vary but can be considerable, depending on the construction crew, how the system goes together, and methods used for fastening.

Movable Partitions

Movable partitions, when properly designed and selected, and when used with a system of workstation standards that respects the structure in which the partitions are to be used, will provide the greatest potential for flexibility and the greatest ease of reconfiguration whenever it is required. This type of partition, when properly used, will require the least amount of labor cost for reconfiguration and the least amount of productivity loss due to downtime, and as the result of distraction during changeover.

Movable partitions ideally will be sized in fractions of the building module (full module, three-quarters module, half-module, or quarter module). Since the majority of new buildings will reflect, to a greater or lesser degree, the 48 or 60 inch (1219 or 1524 mm) dimensions to which material manufacturers adhere, the sizes (in inches or mm) will be as follows:

Building Module	Full Module	Three-quarter Module	Half Module	One-Quarter Module
48 (1219)	48 (1219)	36 (914)	24 (607)	12 (305)
60 (1524)	60 (1524)	45 (1143)	30 (762)	15 (381)

These partitions may be easily attached to the ceiling grid without causing damage to the grid or its finish and it is important that the partitions can be adequately anchored at the floor, regardless of finish, without penetrating the floor finish. It is highly desirable that the system be nonprogressive, that is, that it be so designed as to allow exchanging panels without having to disturb other panels not directly involved in the exchange (i.e., substitute a door panel or a glazed panel in place of a solid panel without removing panels on either side of the one being removed).

MOVABLE SCREENS

Movable screens are available in three different types and functional capabilities.

Systems Furniture

Movable screens can be a component part of a manufacturer's system furniture package; these will support various other components, such as worksurfaces and various storage shelves, bins, or drawers. These screens may also allow the attachments and use of various accessories such as white boards, tack surfaces, and paper flow management devices.

Sight Barrier—Minimum Support

Movable screens can be primarily free-standing sight screens; these have the capability to support usually a very limited number of shelves or bins when used in specific configurations. These screens require the use of free-standing desks, tables, and so on for worksurfaces. These screens normally have a limited sound-attenuating capability.

Sight Barrier Only

Movable screens can be intended for use only as sight screens; these have no other intended use. These screens will not support storage or worksurface components.

WORKMODULES

A workmodule is composed of the various furniture and equipment items that are necessary to support performance of the job description by the individual to whom it is assigned.

Without a workmodule all an individual has is space. It may be open or enclosed space but it is just space. Obviously before work can be performed an employee must have a workmodule as well. Workmodules are necessary for every person from entry level clerk to chairman of the board. The workmodule includes every piece of furniture, systems furniture, furnishings, equipment, and every accessory needed for the individual worker to perform the tasks required of the job description that he or she is assigned.

All items that are part of the workmodule are not required directly for functional execution of the work. Some furnishings are provided to make the individual more productive by removing fatigue factors, and in some cases health hazards. Making workers more comfortable, in most instances, benefits the organization as much or more than the individual worker. Such is true when appropriate and effective wrist supports are provided for use by persons doing keyboarding tasks as a precaution against carpal tunnel syndrome. In this particular kind of situation the individuals are made more comfortable while at the same time having their health protected. Another example is the furnishing of a footrest, where the need is indicated. Each of these factors adds to improved productivity and profit potential.

MODULAR CARPET

Modular carpet, also known as carpet tiles or carpet squares, is the result of efforts by a European carpet manufacturer to utilize waste manufacturing materials. In dynamic organizations of today, modular carpet is being used because it affords a multitude of opportunities for flexibility, extended carpet life, and access to underfloor or undercarpet utilities with an attractive, cost-effective material.

Not many years ago the average life of commercial carpet was about 5 years. Also a fact at that time, on average at time of replacement, 10 percent of the carpet in an installation was worn out, but 100 percent was thrown away. The worn portion of course was in high traffic areas such as aisles and corridors. There were usually a few unsightly areas that were burnt, stained, or were otherwise damaged, but for the most part the carpet looked nice, providing that it had been maintained properly and providing also that the carpet had some quality to begin with.

Modular carpet was originally made in Europe by imbedding animal hair or yarn fiber by needlepunching it into an asphalt backing material, cutting it precisely into squares from 18 to 30 inches (457 mm to 762 mm), or larger, and cementing them into place. The appearance of the animal hair carpet made in Europe was too utilitarian for most American carpet users. American manufacturers began to manufacture modular carpet, also, using mostly synthetic yarns and using generally some type of vinyl plastic backing materials.

Size

Modular carpet has a number of features. Features that relate to function begin when the carpet is shipped from the mill. Broadloom carpet, normally 12 feet (3.66 m) wide, is shipped in rolls that are 12 feet (3.66 m) long, 3 feet (0.91 m) or more in diameter, and weigh hundreds of pounds (kilos) per roll. The size and weight require special equipment to load and unload the carpet from the trucks. For buildings that do not have freight or other elevators with removable ceiling panels, the carpet rolls must be carried on top of the elevator cab, or slung beneath the cab to carry it to building floors above the first or ground level. In some instances corridors are also difficult to negotiate. These difficulties translate into higher installation costs.

Modular carpet is shipped from the mill in cartons measuring approximately 18¼ inches (464 mm) wide by 18¼ inches (464 mm) deep by 6¼ inches (159 mm) high, and contain 5 square yards (4 square meters) of carpet. These cartons are easy to handle and may be stacked as high as space and weight regulations will allow. The same kind of handling ease is evident when loading and unloading freight elevators or passenger elevators that are used alternately for freight. If necessary these cartons can be carried up stairs with no more difficulty than one normally encounters with cartons of the same size and weight.

Installation

Installation of modular carpet in a new building or space may be scheduled after other trades have completed their work, avoiding the potential for soiling and damage. This results in the saving of time and money.

Yarn Problems

With face yarn securely fastened into the backing material of modular carpet, either by fusion bonding or other processes to accomplish the same attachment assurance, well-known carpet problems associated with much broadloom carpet is nonexistent. These include edge raveling, delamination, yarn pulls, and stretching.

Carpet Life Extension

Every carpet installation has areas that are used by a large number of the people in the area in addition to those who are just passing through. Eventually, depending on number of people walking on the carpet, how often they walk on it, the original quality of the carpet, and the degree of maintenance and cleaning the carpet receives, any carpet will begin to show signs of wear. With broadloom carpet the normal course is to allow deterioration to continue to a point where the decision is made to replace the carpet.

With modular carpet you have the option to rotate, or exchange the carpet in areas of high traffic with other carpet areas that experience medium, low, and no traffic. This rotation is relatively inexpensive to accomplish and will extend the life of the total carpet installation considerably. Replacement of tiles that have cigarette or other burns, stains, or other types of damage is also a simple matter consisting of using a tile from under a desk or file to replace one that is burnt, stained, or otherwise damaged. The result of such rotation is an extended carpet life that averages 12 years, compared to an average life for broadloom of 7 years.

Free Lay with Only Adhesive Control Grid

A properly designed and manufactured carpet tile does not need adhesive to keep it in place. The weight and design of the tile backing will cause it to maintain contact with the floor without the use of adhesive. An adhesive grid placed at 30 feet center-to-center in both directions will control the carpet and prevent building and other vibrations from moving the carpet across the floor. A carpet tile that will dome (raise up in the center) or cup (raise up at the corners or edges) without the use of adhesive should not be used. Such problems indicate a lack of adequate stability in the backing.

System Furniture Areas—Simplified Replacement

Some of the greatest savings to be obtained by using modular carpet are those realized when it is time to reconfigure your workplace. Since carpet tiles do not all have to be removed at the same time, there is less disruption of the workers. Disconnection and reconnection of power, telephones, and computer cables can be virtually eliminated. Systems furniture can be moved without dismantling completely and the same is true of various other pieces of office equipment.

Easily Cleaned

Carpet tiles are easy to clean and maintain on site on the floor, or off-site. Tiles may be easily removed to a remote off-site area for cleaning.

THE FLEXIBLE FLOOR

A flexible floor, like a flexible ceiling, provides a high degree of flexibility as relates to accessing the utilities and various forms of cabling that are required to be located at various points throughout the workplace.

There two types of accessibility that the raised accessible floor provides. First, there is the accessibility to the water, air, electrical power, telephone, and data cables for the the computer network. This allows the specific pipes, flexible ducts, and cables, including fiber optic, to be relocated with relative ease. Second, there is the opportunity to locate various valves, switches, outlets, and connectors on top of the floor, at the specific location where each must be if it is to be available for the final connection of the computer, typewriter, calculator, or other equipment that is to be used by each individual worker.

Accessible Raised Floor

The accessible floor is composed of square panels, 24 inches square (607 mm square) to 30 inches square (762 mm square) and may be made of metal, wood products, or even cement. The panels are supported by adjustable supports at each corner. Each support carries one corner from each of four contiguous floor panels. The distance from the supporting building floor to the bottom of the accessible raised floor panel may be anywhere from approximately 6 inches (152 mm) to about 24 inches (607mm).

Finishes for the top of raised accessible floors vary. Some are furnished with hard surfaces for clean rooms or areas, some with resilient materials such as vinyl sheet material, and some with carpet. Whatever the material it must meet electrostatic dissipative (ESD) standards for use in computer rooms or other areas where static electric build-ups cannot be tolerated. In addition, modular carpet can be used over the accessible floor inasmuch as the accessibility of the floor is not diminished since the modular carpet allows access to the floor panels and the space beneath it. The same ESD parameters apply.

THE COST—THE PAYBACK

There are two very important points to remember when it comes to getting your capital investment back and when it comes to reaping the thousands and thousands of dollars of additional profit that can be yours as a result of the Beta solution described herein.

The furniture, the systems furniture, the building materials, and the finish materials that we recommend in this book are all cost effective when used as described, and when properly specified, furnished, constructed, and installed.

Virtually every material or item that is cost effective has a premium first cost, particularly if there is a short payback period.

As with other cost-effective equipment or materials, the cost advantages do not stop when the payback has been completed. The savings continue and result in profit potential for the organization (see Appendix A, Table 1).

LOGISTICS

There are a number of factors that contribute to the efficiency of managing the workplace and that simplify the logistics of the inventory.

Two factors in particular are related to the size and color of systems furniture panels and components. From a logistical position, having all panels the same single light neutral color ensures that the panels that are in your inventory are finished in the color you need for your next workplace reconfiguration. Another benefit of a single light neutral color for panels relates to reduced energy costs. Panels finished as described above can effectively reduce the amount of light necessary to adequately illuminate the workplace. This is another saving that contributes to an increased profit.

The fewer sizes of panels you use the more likely you are to have the size panel you need to add or reconfigure parts of your workplace as the need arises. The vertical heights for panels you will need are as follows:

Panels 42 inches (1067 mm) high for receptionists and other individuals who must greet people and/or otherwise have need of a transaction shelf as they work with visitors or other workers.

Panels 62 to 66 inches (1575 to 1676 mm) high for clerks, secretaries, supervisors, engineers, and accountants.

Panels 75 to 84 inches (1905 to 2134 mm) high for first and second line managers. Positions above this level, depending on the job description, may need to be enclosed with full height movable and/or full height fixed partitions.

Limiting the number of different panel widths used in your workplace will make a difference also. Generally it is good to have a full-module panel, a half-module panel, and a panel 24 to 25 inches (607 to 635 mm) wide, which is used for sight cut-off on workmodules one and two, as part of your standards and your inventory. The panel widths you will need are as follows:

If your facility is built on a 60-inch (1524-mm) module the full-module panel will be 60 inches (1524 mm) wide and the half-module panel will be 30 inches (762 mm) wide, plus the 24 inch (607 mm) panel.

If your facility is built on a 48-inch (1219-mm) module the full-module panel will be 48 inches (1219 mm) wide and the half-module panel will be 24 inches (607 mm) wide, and will also serve as the additional panel described above.

If your facility has a module other than the standard 48 or 60 inch (1219 or 1524 mm), it will be necessary to create unique standards that respond to the module of your building or to superimpose either the 48- or 60-inch (1219-mm or 1524-mm) module grid over the floor plan of your facility. This can be done whether you have a single structure or several structures.

Limiting the number of different lengths of systems furniture components (shelves, binder bins, files, worksurfaces, etc.) is likewise important to the efficient management of the workplace. Smaller dimensions can provide greater flexibility, although at a greater initial cost. As an example, it costs less (as much as 26 percent less) to purchase a single 60-inch (1524-mm)-wide panel rather than two 30-inch (762-mm)-wide panels. The advantage, however, is that with two 30-inch (762-mm) panels you can then solve the need for one 30-inch (762-mm) panel, or one 60-inch (1524-mm) panel, or a need for two 30-inch (762-mm) panels. Conversely with a single 60-inch (1524-mm) panel you are able to solve only the need for one 60-(1524-mm) inch panel—three solutions versus one. The same amount of space is required for storage. This is essentially true for flipper door units (30 percent less cost). With worksurfaces there can actually be a savings if two smaller units are purchased. The cost is actually greater (about 4 percent) to purchase the larger length. Cost comparisons may change and may not apply to the products of all manufacturers; it is worth considering, however.

THE SHUMAKE BETA MODULE

The Shumake Beta Module was developed in response to the need to have large numbers of clerical workers in a high density configuration and still maintain a minimal factor of inadvertent distraction. Additional goals were to reduce fatigue factors and to reduce the feeling of being confined in a tiny *cage*, *pod*, or *cubicle*.

The ability to consistently respond to the above needs and to consistently achieve the above goals requires that deterrents be addressed in order that they may be reduced or removed completely. To accomplish such results requires use of the basic workmodule configuration and worker orientation indicated in Figure 10.1.

Working from the base any size workstation and workmodule can be accommodated (see Figure 10.3).

The Beta Module is the base core for all workmodules whether for the entry level clerk or the chairman of the board. The reason that the Beta Module base core is necessary for all workmodules is simply that the workers who will use them are all humans, each with all of the abilities and limitations that the majority of humans in the developed world have in common.

The Beta Module, in addition to constituting the base core for all work modules, is also a complete workmodule. It is designated W-1B, which indicates workmodule-1B (the *B* designates base). The 60-inch by 60-inch (1524-mm by 1524-mm) dimensioned square of space has a net area of 25 square feet (2.25

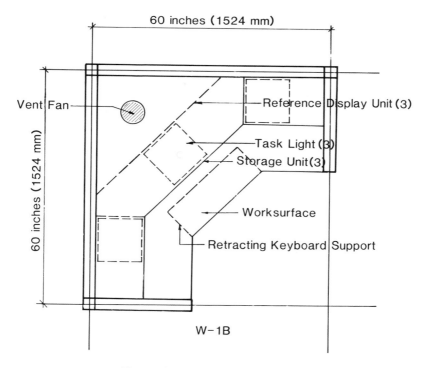

Figure 10.1. Shumake Beta Module.

square meters). This is the largest net area that can be justified on the basis of functional efficiency with two exceptions. The first exception is for any worker whose tasks require that the worker meet, in their workstation, with outside visitors or other workers. The other exception is to provide for more than the normal amount of storage within the workstation proper.

The dimensions of this workmodule are such that the overwhelming majority of healthy individuals without a physical handicap can reach virtually all parts of the worksurfaces, storage units, and reference display units from the primary seated work position. This can be accomplished by merely rotating the workmodule chair (see Figure 10.2).

All worksurfaces must be adjustable vertically by 1 inch increments (2.54 centimeters) to compensate for variations in the distance from the floor to the underside of an individual's thigh when they are seated. When the primary task is keyboarding and the terminal has a detached keyboard the corner worksurface must also have a retractable keyboard support, either in the form of a drawer, or an articulating support mechanism. As we stated previously, it is important that the worksurface finish be light in color to reduce contrast between the surface and the work materials that will be placed thereon.

Included in the Beta Module are two types of storage areas. The first is made up of three shelf units mounted to the panels above the worksurface. The portion of the shelf that is located directly above the corner worksurface may be

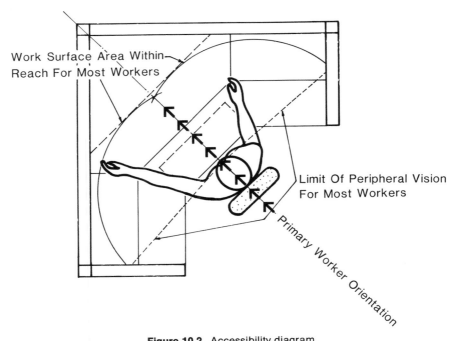

Figure 10.2. Accessibility diagram.

open or closed and is lockable. To either side of the corner storage unit are standard flipper door storage units, also with locks. This storage area is used to store all active files used by the individual in addition to active binders and other bound or bindered storage devices. The second storage area is located beneath the worksurface and is used to store small office supplies in the two upper 6-inch drawers; the lower 12-inch drawer is for personal items such as shoes, lunches, or newspaper. Any item that is accessed more than one time per day must not be located beneath the worksurface. It is too costly to access.

Tackable reference areas are continuous around the interior perimeter of the workmodule. Adjustable task lights are located to either side of the corner storage unit and provide task illumination where needed. A small vent fan is located in the corner storage module and draws air from the workmodule interior at the corner and exhausts it to the ambient air space above the workstation. Power, telephone, and data cables are accessed at desk height where needed in the workmodule. Paperflow management items and other accessories are available for use as necessary.

FUNCTION VERSUS STATUS

As previously stated the Shumake Beta Module measures 60 inches (1524 mm square and has an area of 25 net square feet (2.25 square meters) of floor space. Twenty five net square feet (2.25 square meters) is the largest amount of area that can be correctly assigned for most individuals based on the need for functional efficiency. This statement has to do with the fact that with few exceptions workers cannot reach beyond this distance when measured from and to either side of the center line of the primary work position.

The statement does not indicate that a workstation cannot have more than 25 net square feet (2.25 square meters) of floor space. It means that any space in the workstation in addition to the stated amount is for some reason other than functional efficiency. There are two exceptions to this rule. A workstation will need additional area for conference needs, and for extraordinary files or other storage or special equipment that must be located within that workstation.

Normally there are one, two, or three parts to a clerical workstation and workmodule. A supervisor's workstation and workmodule will have three parts. Every workmodule has the following:

1. The functional part that contains the primary work area (see Figure 10.3). Sometimes a clerical or supervisor's workstation and workmodule will also have
2. an excess storage and/or equipment area and/or
3. a visitor's chair.

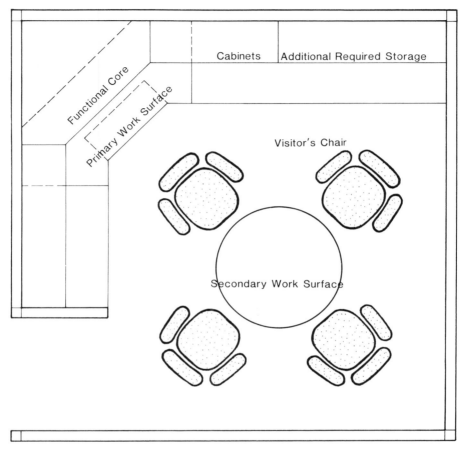

Figure 10.3. Diagram showing parts of workstation.

There are normally either three or four parts to a manager's or an executive's workstation and workmodule. Every workmodule has

1. The functional part, which contains the primary work area, and
2. a second functional part, which contains the secondary work area (conference). Some workmodules will also have
3. an excess storage and equipment area and/or
4. a status area (informal conference, formal conference, bar, etc.).

There are occasionally exceptional situations that have to do with building constraints. Most often the reason additional space is included in workstations is for purposes of status. Bigger is normally perceived as better and since function plays no part in such a perception, the added space *is* the enhancement; *the added space provides the status.*

There are other situations in which functional provisions are viewed as being provided for purposes of status. An example is the informal conference area in the office of an executive or manager. The same perception may be applied to a formal conference area in or attached to the office of another manager or executive. In the extreme there will be offices that have both formal and informal conference areas that are both functional and appropriate because of the type of meetings that are held there and the clients who attend them. Of course, there will always be those executives who have those amenities simply because they want them, and because they have the *power* to have them.

II

THE PRODUCTIVE WORKPLACE: WHAT IT TAKES!

INTRODUCTION TO PART II

The problem has been identified and defined and the solution has been outlined. Following hereafter is a detailed program of attack for use by management in an effort to provide the optimum workplace where white- and gold-collar workers will have the opportunity to perform their particular assignments with a near maximum potential for productivity.

11

WORKSTATIONS AND WORKMODULES

Just as there needs to be a job description for each individual, there is a need also for a standard to support that job description. A standard consists of a workstation, which is a territorial assignment, and a work module, which consists of the specific furniture, furnishings, and equipment necessary for performance of the various tasks required by the job description. The majority of organizations can be serviced by general categories for workstation standards as shown in Table 11.1.

WORKSTATION STANDARDS

There may be any number of variations to these standards, as determined by the requirements of the job description, for storage and equipment, It is important, if the standards are to be controlled, that the classifications, first, be limited in number, and then monitored, maintained, and adhered to.

Originally, standards are to be set up to accommodate every existing job description in the organization, plus any new job descriptions that are being added at that time, if any. As new positions are created, new job descriptions will be written to describe the work tasks that are expected of the individuals who will fill those particular positions. It is important that a workstation and workmodule standard also be assigned at the same time, to support the tasks of the new job description. It is entirely possible that an existing standard will serve the functional needs of the tasks perfectly. No assumption as to the correctness of this possibility should be made, however. The workstation and workmodule for the job description must be determined through a thorough evaluation of the tasks required, and the furniture, furnishings, and equipment that are necessary and that will allow the worker to function as efficiently as possible and with inadvertent distractions and fatigue reduced to the lowest amounts possible.

TABLE 11.1. Workstation Standards

Workstation Standard	Classification	Space Allocation
1.0	Clerical	20.50–56.25 sq ft (1.85–5.06 sq m)
2.0	Clerical w/visitor	41.00–56.25 sq ft (3.69–5.06 sq m)
3.0	Supervisor	56.25–100.00 sq ft (5.06–9.00 sq m)
4.0	A—Manager	100.00–144.00 sq ft (9.00–12.96 sq m)
5.0	B—Manager	150.00–192.00 sq ft (13.50–17.28 sq m)
6.0	C—Manager	225.00–256.00 sq ft (20.25–23.04 sq m)
7.0	D—Exec	300.00–320.00 sq ft (27.00–28.80 sq m)
8.0	E—Exec	400.00 sq ft (36.00 sq m)
9.0	F—Exec	Varies with accommodations
10.0	Special purpose	Varies according to use and need

The creation of a new standard is best accomplished by an experienced facilities person, or a knowledgeable and experienced consultant, together with a supervisor who is experienced in the group where the work will be performed, and who has knowledge of the work or of work that is similar to the work that is required by the new job description. Based on the work required, estimates will be prepared to determine the following:

The probable quantity of incoming work materials, the size, composition, and format of the material, and where the material will be placed and stored until worked on.

Where will the materials likely be placed while being worked on?

In addition to the materials actually being worked on, what reference and other materials will likely be used simultaneously, as part of the work process? What is the size of each? Where will these additional items be placed while being worked with or on?

What will be the quantity, size, and composition of completed materials from this station? Where does it go from here? Where will it be placed until it leaves this station? What is the maximum normal accumulation that may be expected until it is moved to the next workstation?

What will be the size and quantity of material that will be held in the station while waiting for information, additional material, or a specific date before being completed and sent on to the next station for further processing or completion?

Are there any periods with abnormally large amounts of work materials to be processed? How will these larger amounts be handled and stored while in the workstation?

What equipment, standard or special, will be necessary to perform the tasks of the job description? All needs must be evaluated, large or small, frequent or occasional.

Will the storage or equipment needs of this workstation be large enough to be considered abnormal to the point that more than the normal equipment and/or storage capability will be required for purposes of functional efficiency?

What about a need for isolation? What will be the conference needs for this job description? Will the information that will be discussed, stored, or passing through this station be of a sensitive or confidential nature? Will any need for confidentiality be visual, aural, or both?

What are the proximity needs for this job description? With whom will they likely meet, where, and how often? With whom of the in-house staff, supervisors, management, and executives must they speak in person for whatever reason? Where and how often?

A standard Shumake Beta Module provides for the needs of virtually all clerical, supervisory, management, and executive white-collar information-processing functions. By expanding this base core, any information-processing function can be accommodated completely so that the tasks required may be performed efficiently with a minimum of inadvertent distraction and fatigue.

Special Requirements Equal Temporary Standard

Special requirements for an individual should be dealt with as a temporary variation to a workstation standard for a particular classification. This holds true whether the need for variance is due to function or expedience.

Example (function): A record clerk has a need to maintain files containing 6,000 linear inches of records. Further it is known that because of a continuing conversion to electronic storage the need for this amount of hard copy storage will all but vanish within 3 years.

It is obvious that such a large number of files cannot be contained in the territory assigned to a Category 1.0, File Clerk. Instead of creating a new category to accommodate the situation, a variation is made to Category 1.0. The new variation becomes as follows: 1.1 Clerk, Special File. This variation is considered temporary and is maintained only for as long as the need exists.

Example (expediency): At the time standards assignments become effective, a manager of long and loyal standing has been occupying an office clearly above his category. The office was "inherited" from his predecessor when the manager took over the duties of the previous officer. He has not been elevated to the same rank, since his job description is only a part of the prior officer's duties. The manager is to retire within a relatively short period of time and management decides to leave the manager in the office until such retirement.

Instead of creating a new category for the situation, and instead of assigning a more prestigious category that sets a precedent that may create more problems in the future, a variation is made to Category 4.0. The new category becomes as follows: 4.1 Manager, Special Condition. This variation, also, is considered temporary and should be maintained only for as long as the need exists. The category list should be reviewed and purged of obsolete variations no less than once each year.

WORKSTATIONS

A workstation, as previously stated, is a space or territory assigned to an individual for use while performing the tasks required by their particular job function. It is nothing more than an assignment of space. The workstation for an executive or manager may be surrounded by full height partitions. A supervisor may be assigned a space in the center of a large area, hopefully surrounded by screens, and be further surrounded by other spaces that are assigned to individuals who are to be supervised.

The term workstation is frequently used in reference to a space plus the furniture and equipment contained therein. If there is to be an organized and systemized method of managing the interior spaces of the white-collar workplace, and if management expects to be able to maintain both flexibility and control of the facility, it is necessary and desirable to have a means by which it is easy to identify and support the variety of tasks required by the job descriptions.

The term workstation then is used to describe the assignment of space; the term workmodule is used to describe and reference that particular combination of furniture, systems furniture, furnishings, equipment, and accessories necessary that supports a particular job description, taking into account all of the task variations for each individual worker.

WORKMODULES

Workmodules, like standards, may have a large number of variations. Since the workmodule consists of a specific combination of furniture, equipment, and accessories that supports a particular job description, it will also reflect the differences between job descriptions by containing only those items of furniture, furnishings, equipment, and accessories that are required to support the tasks that are assigned to that unique job description.

There are workmodules that will support many different job descriptions. This is due to the fact that although the type of work is similar, the tasks may be altogether different. The storage needs may be larger or smaller, or different materials or media may be used. The importance of making the workmodule support the tasks of the job description, and of adjusting the workmodule to fit the individual who will be assigned to it cannot be stressed too strongly. Each time a different person is assigned to a particular workmodule, the fit should be checked by facility people or the organization that they use to reconfigure the space. If the fit is right, do not change it. If the fit is not correct, adjust it until it is. Remember, your company's profitability depends in part on that fit being correct.

The individual who is assigned the responsibility, or who has the responsibility, for monitoring the workplace must be someone who understands the Beta concept and who is sold on what it can do for the organization and for every white-collar worker who works for the organization.

For each individual there are three assignments.

1. Job Description
2. Workstation
3. Workmodule

Example: Individual A has the following job description (simplified): 1.50 Clerk, Mail.

Duties consist of: Pick up from post office, sorting and delivering incoming U.S. mail. Pick up from individuals, sorting and delivering in-house mail. Maintaining postage meter and obtaining postage for same when necessary. Receive, seal, stamp, sort, and bundle outgoing U.S. mail and deliver to post office before 6:00 PM each work day.

Example: Individual B has the following job description (simplified): 1.51 Clerk, Mail.

Duties consist of: Pick up from post office, sorting and delivering incoming U.S. mail. Pick up from individuals, sorting and delivering in-house mail. Maintaining postage meter and obtaining postage for same when necessary. Receive, seal, stamp, sort, and bundle outgoing U.S. mail and deliver to post office before 6:00 PM each work day. Maintain mailing list of all company offices, adding and deleting names, daily, as indicated on status change reports.

The duties of the job descriptions in the preceding examples are identical except for a single task: that of maintaining the mailing list. Clearly one position requires the use of a typewriter or input device and the other does not. Each would require the same standard, the same workstation, but a different workmodule. The latter workmodule would include a typewriter or input device, the former would not.

SUPPORT MODULES

Support modules consist of equipment that is for use by more than one person, and the list of furniture and equipment in this category can be extensive. A copier is an example of a support module. The module will normally include a stand for the equipment to be placed on and a storage cabinet for storing supplies for the copier. A support module is made up of shared equipment. A shared phone is a support module. Group or department files constitute a support module and a coat rack is, or is part of, a support module.

UTILIZATION AREA

The utilization area is that area required in front of, on the side of, in back of, or around a piece of furniture or equipment in order to use it, work at it, repair it, or maintain it. For example, to be able to use a standard letter file, it is necessary to open the drawer. To open the drawer there must be enough space in front of the file for the drawer to open without hitting an object and/or without blocking a passageway. In addition there must be room for the person using the file to stand, also out of the passageway, while they perform tasks at the file (see Figure 11.1).

A worktable may be completely in the open, in the center of the room or area with space on all sides to work. The utilization area is on all sides as well. If the same table is located against a wall, but without a wall, other furniture, or equipment at either end, it may be used, or *utilized* by someone along the entire long edge or at either end. The utilization area is along those three edges of the table, and so forth. There are managers and designers who neglect to allow utilization space for the furniture and equipment they intend to place in various spaces, then find themselves in spaces that have virtually no access space since it has by necessity become utilization space.

SPECIAL FUNCTION WORKMODULES

A special function workmodule is made up of the furniture and equipment assigned to a single individual, where the operation of that equipment is the primary task of the individual. Examples of this type of workmodule will be found in the print shop, the computer room, and the mail room (see Ancillary Areas). In such areas there will normally be found support modules as well.

The distinction between the workmodule and the special function workmodule is the specialized nature of the function. The workmodule has equipment and furniture that is used for many similar, but different, office functions while the special function workmodule equipment usually is used for a specific, limited function, or a group of related functions.

There are certain kinds of equipment that may be found in both categories, although models will be different as necessitated by greater or lesser work loads. Copiers are one example of a crossover category. A smaller copier will be used as a support module for a department or group. A large production copier will be used in the reproduction or printing department of many organizations.

ACCESS AND EGRESS

How easily people can get into and out of your workplace is of a varying degree of concern to certain departments of government. More specifically your local municipality or county, more often than not, is concerned with how easily and safely all people, but particularly handicapped people, can get from outside your workspace into it, through it as necessary, and back outside again in every situation, and especially during a fire or natural disaster, should one occur.

What this means to you generally, since only an inspection and advice from your own building and fire officials will tell you for certain, is that attention must be paid to all parts of your workplace. Building codes in most areas regulate the physical size of your entire building and most if not all of the spaces that make up your building. The same codes regulate what materials may be used to construct your building as well as when and how certain of the materials may be used, if at all. These codes regulate door widths and types, the widths of all passageways, aisles, and corridors; maximum lengths of dead-end passageways, aisles, and corridors; and the installation and maintenance of required exit lights. If you are not the building owner you may bear responsibility for only the layout of your own interior space. This includes any construction you cause to be installed to create permanent or movable partitions as well as the aisles created by your conventional or systems furniture.

As a result of your interior layout, additional exit lights may be required. In addition, some type of emergency lighting system is required by building or life safety codes in most areas. Such a system includes emergency lighting units that turn on automatically when the normal power for lighting is disrupted for any reason. The light from these units provides illumination for workers and others as they leave the workplace during the emergency.

Having this type of automatic lighting in place can prevent panic and injury during an emergency. If a system of emergency lighting is not required by law, it is certainly recommended as a means of preventing injury or death, and will normally reduce the organization's liability when your company has an emergency situation that is caused by or that results in a power outage.

In July 1990 the American with Disabilities Act (ADA) was passed by the Congress of the United States and signed by the President. It is now law and affects every business in the United States in some way or other.

Toilet facilities, again particularly for the handicapped, have come increasingly under scrutiny of government building departments and the building codes they enforce. In addition to requiring a certain number and type of toilets, urinals, and wash basins, the code may very well dictate special sizes of fixtures and enclosures for some of those required. This is to ensure access by disabled individuals.

To ignore the requirements of these building and fire department officials is to run the risk of not being able to move into your workplace once it is completed. In many localities an occupancy permit is required, which, simply

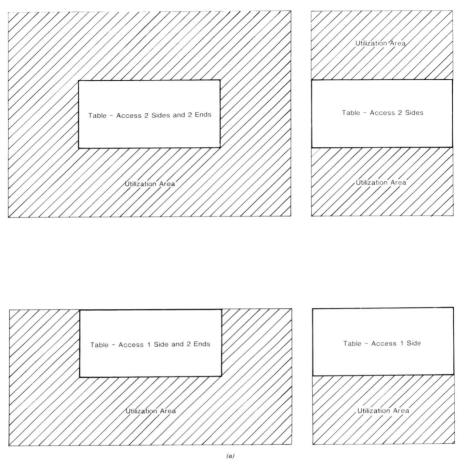

Figure 11.1. Utilization areas.

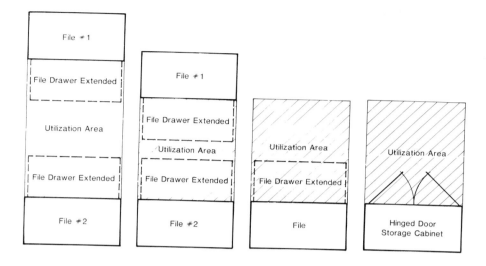

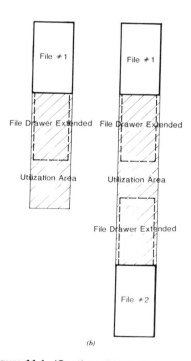

(b)

Figure 11.1. (*Continued*) Utilization areas.

stated, attests to the fact that you have complied with the ordinances and codes of that particular jurisdiction. Until you have your occupancy permit you will not be allowed to move in.

A rather large midwestern corporation was ready to move into their new downtown headquarters. Someone had failed to be certain that a particular new type of wall covering that was being used on the walls of the executive offices would pass a flammability test called a small scale vertical burn. The fabric would not pass the test when a flame was applied to the test fabric by a local fire official. Later when the executives tried to move into their new offices, they found that the fire department had sealed off the executive area and refused to allow the company officers to enter. Whereupon they were forced to look elsewhere for a place to work temporarily.

Fortunately a vendor with a great deal of experience with wall and wall coverings suggested that if a different, more comprehensive flammability test were used, the fabric would be shown to be safe for use as intended. The fire officials agreed, the test was conducted, the assembly with the material applied passed the alternate test, the occupancy permit was issued, and the executives moved into their new offices. Many materials would not have passed either flammability test and the story would have had a much different ending.

Without such an occupancy permit document, you may find your space or building sealed by one or more of the departments involved, and you will not be allowed to enter or use any, or part of your space until it is brought into compliance with the applicable codes and ordinances.

CORE AREAS

Core areas of a building are those areas that enclose such spaces as mechanical equipment for the building, elevators, toilet areas, elevators, and stairways. In core areas are also found duct shafts and pipe chases. These are vertical spaces connecting one floor to another through which heating, ventilating, and air conditioning ducts are run. Shafts and chases are used also for pipes for the building plumbing, electric conduit, data cable, phone lines, and fire protection systems in buildings that have them. There may be a single central core or there may be several core areas depending on the size and configuration of the building.

A principal concern for productivity improvement involves the acoustical treatment of core walls facing into the workplace. Core walls are some of the single largest vertical surfaces of any building. As such there is a need to treat these surfaces acoustically to prevent the reflection of airborne sound to reduce the possibility of it becoming a distraction (see Vertical Surfaces, Chapter 3).

ANCILLARY AREAS

Ancillary areas are supplementary areas, and as such contain special function groups or services. Among these are mail, printing, reproduction, supply, communications, closed circuit television production studios, and copy centers. Others include reception areas, waiting areas, conference centers, product display areas, libraries, special presentation centers, auditoriums, private washroom facilities, employee lounges, cafeterias, and other dining facilities.

12

OBTAINING THE INFORMATION

When an architect, designer, or management consultant says that it is not necessary to survey all of your white-collar workers and that a sample of each group is sufficient, the following questions will probably come to mind: *Who should we survey? Who do we leave out? How do we decide?* How the consultant answers your questions is not important, because anything less than a complete survey of each and every worker in the organization will seriously risk compromising your entire productivity improvement program. If the consultant does not require the indoctrination of every employee, as well as the inclusion of each in the survey and thereby in the entire planning process, you should ask: *How can we ever hope for a successful effort without the input and cooperation of each and every individual of the areas involved?* The answer is, *You can't.*

It is useless for consultants who believe that surveying *sample* groups of workers to even attempt such an orientation or survey of every person. The absence of knowledge concerning the need for and benefits of these important parts of a productivity improvement effort indicates a lack of basic information on the part of the consultant as to what is required for productivity improvement to occur. Further, it raises a question concerning the consultant or consultant group's ability to cause such improvement to happen, particularly as relates to the Beta Sector.

Of extreme importance to a successful endeavor is this imperative: *Everyone Must Participate—Everyone Must Benefit*, at least potentially.

PERCEIVED VERSUS REAL INFORMATION

In virtually every organization there exists two concepts of how the organization operates. One concept reflects all of the directives, memoranda, and other instructions that have been transmitted to the managers, supervisors, and

113

employees during the time the organization has existed. This concept I refer to as the perceived method of operation.

The second concept is the way the organization actually does operate. In reality, directives, orders, and other instructions are received by supervisors and employees, tried, and when successful are implemented. When such directions are found to be unworkable, an alternative way is frequently found by those whose job it is to carry out the task or tasks, and the operation proceeds. Information concerning this revision may never find its way back up the chain of command for various reasons. Since the operations proceed, often no one ever questions whether this is the prescribed procedure. By this concept the organization is not only able to operate, but able to operate successfully as well.

It is essential that as you begin your productivity improvement effort, data be obtained that reflect information depicting the real operating methods. Information that does not describe what is actually happening in the operation is probably incomplete, inaccurate, and in many cases completely incorrect. Needless to say the use of such data for productivity improvement may be a prelude to disaster.

The mass of information required to plan and design the white-collar environment for an organization will include data for from one to thousands of persons. It is important that no matter how large or small the employee population may be, the information obtained include pertinent data about each and every individual to be accommodated in the space or spaces being planned, and that the data be obtained from each individual about themselves and about their workstation and workmodule situation.

INFORMATION ABOUT THE INDIVIDUAL

There is a need for the following information to be included in the data obtained from each individual (see Appendix A).

The first information is relative to the individual's personal identification including name, identification number, department or group, job title, and to whom the worker reports directly. It should also be determined how long that individual has been performing their present assignment and whether the person is left or right handed.

Information must be gathered about materials that the individual has that need to be stored on shelves, in drawers, in cabinets, or in other types of storage units. The type and normal quantities of each kind of material stored in the individual's workstation must be determined. The quantity for most items will be measured in linear inches (linear centimeters).

To help you identify the types of storage normally found in workstations, please refer to Figure 12.1. Refer to Figure 12.2 for information explaining the method to be used when measuring the quantity of material to be stored in individual storage units.

Further information is needed about how the worker works with, and otherwise uses, the materials in the workstation. It is necessary to learn which materials and other items are used on the worksurfaces, the sizes of each kind of material, and the combinations in which these are used at the same time. Data are required regarding the various types of reference books, reference binders, and other reference materials to be stored and used by the individual at their workstation.

Manufacturer's specifications are needed for any machines that are to be located for use on the individual worksurface as well as machines or equipment that are to be located for use within the individual workstation other than on the work surfaces. These specifications are needed so that appropriate power, telephone, and data cable, or any other utilities that may be required can be provided where needed.

It is important to have information relating to how work flows into the individual workstation, how it is processed, if and how it is held for additional work or information, and finally how it is passed on for further work, to be mailed, to be filed, or otherwise disposed of. It is equally important to know the volume of the material that passes through the workstation as well as how long it remains in the station.

Information must be obtained concerning the required use by the individual of shared equipment and services, how often the equipment or service is needed, and the extent of its use. These data are needed for each different type of equipment and/or service needed.

The planner/designer has need for information about the individual's person-to-person communications that are conducted within the employee's own workstation. There is a need for information as to how often meetings are

Shelf Storage

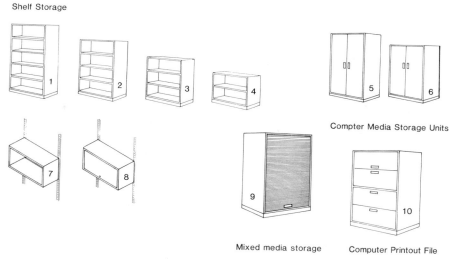

Figure 12.1. Storage types.

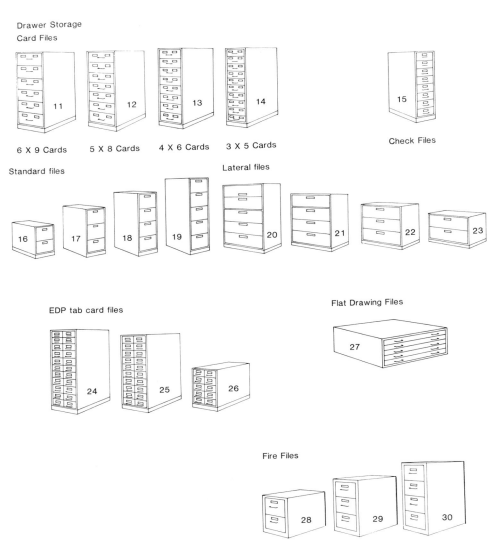

Drawer Storage
Card Files

6 X 9 Cards   5 X 8 Cards   4 X 6 Cards   3 X 5 Cards   Check Files

Standard files   Lateral files

EDP tab card files   Flat Drawing Files

Fire Files

Figure 12.1. (*Continued*)

held there, how many persons, other than the individual, are in these meetings, and how long the meetings last.

It is necessary to have information about the existence of any need for individual isolation, and whether the need is for purposes of confidentiality, concentration, or other reasons. The key word here is need as opposed to want.

The above information, once gathered for each employee, provides a specific reference that provides the basis on which all individual workmodules are formulated. This information allows the facility planners and managers, with

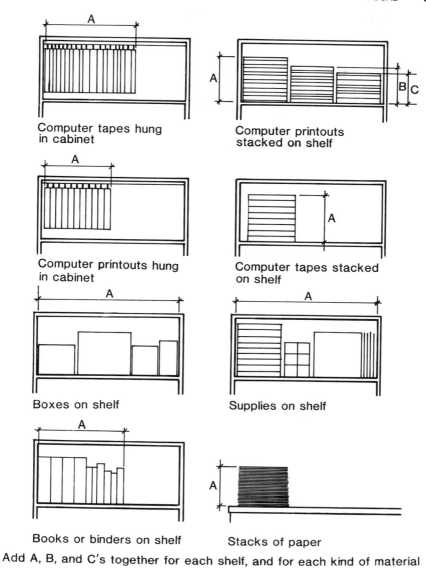

Computer tapes hung
in cabinet

Computer printouts
stacked on shelf

Computer printouts hung
in cabinet

Computer tapes stacked
on shelf

Boxes on shelf

Supplies on shelf

Books or binders on shelf   Stacks of paper

Add A, B, and C's together for each shelf, and for each kind of material

(a)

Figure 12.2. How to measure quantities of work materials.

their consultants, to provide an optimized workplace—a workplace where the working environment is healthier and more pleasant for the individual workers, and a workplace that makes it easier for employees to do the tasks required of them. The same workplace provides reduced operating costs as a result of increased individual productivity. Increased profit is the result of increased productivity.

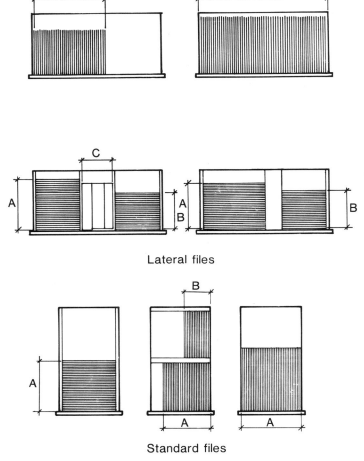

Lateral files

Standard files

Add A, B, and C's together for each drawer, and for each kind of material

(b)

Figure 12.2. *(Continued)*

INFORMATION ABOUT SHARED FURNITURE AND EQUIPMENT

In addition to information about the individual's own workstation, it is also necessary to obtain information about all other parts of the space. This includes materials, equipment, and machines that are shared by more than one individual. Simply stated the goal of information gathering is to account for everyone and everything once and no individual or no item of furniture, furnishings, or equipment more than once.

Information to be gathered about shared furniture, equipment, machines, and so on, includes the following.

Collect information concerning storage on shelves, in drawers, in hinged door cabinets and in file cabinets of every configuration, either currently in use, or needed to be used. The data that are to be collected will document what needs to be stored and how much there is to store.

If present storage units are to be reused, an inventory will be needed. The inventory should not be confused with the surveys that are referred to in this chapter. The surveys help to determine what kind of storage is needed and how much. Inventories merely record what kind of storage and other kinds of furniture and equipment presently exist, and where it is presently located.

It is desirable to know whether any type of special storage is required. If so, determine particulars relating to such special storage and document.

Additionally it is important to know if and to what extent any storage requirements are changing. Are they increasing, decreasing, or remaining constant?

Determine if any special use or work areas are needed. Find out what are they and what the criteria is for each?

Gather information about the conference needs of the group, department, or entire organization, depending on what portion of the company is being surveyed.

Determine if there exists any need for isolation, for whatever reason, of any group.

It is important to identify and to separate individual or group needs from individual or group wants. Need indicates necessity, or those things that are essential to perform functional tasks required by the job description. Want, on the other hand, indicates desire, or those things that the individual or group would like to have. Also there may actually be a perceived need that cannot be shown to be real.

As an example, consider as a need a typewriter for someone whose job description requires that he or she type invoices. A want might be a sophisticated, expensive memory typewriter for the same person.

There are many gray areas where wanted equipment might actually improve the productivity potential of a particular employee. Having identified such a desire by the individual or group to have the item for their use is sufficient. This then becomes an area requiring review and study by the organization to determine the desirability, cost effectiveness, and so on, of acquiring the furniture, equipment, or whatever the item happens to be.

No indication as to the probability of such item being procured should ever be made to the worker by anyone other than those individuals of management that have the authority to request or to authorize the procurement.

13

ANALYZING THE DATA

Most of those who work in offices are familiar with the normal methods of storage for the individual as well as shared storage for groups or departments.

When using the "Beta Module" as the core of all workstations for part of the improvement in the white-collar environment, workstation storage must be provided in a relatively specific manner for some of the benefits to be realized. It is partially to that end that accurate storage requirements need to be determined, as described in the preceding chapter, no matter what systems furniture you choose, or are already using.

Once the data have been obtained, however, it must be analyzed and a summary prepared. Provision must be made to accommodate those materials and other items for which storage is needed. Work surfaces and reference areas required by the task functions of each individual job description must also be provided. Equipment that is to be used in the workstation, either on the worksurface or on the floor, must be accommodated.

INDIVIDUAL STORAGE AND EQUIPMENT

Information obtained from the survey documents will indicate how much storage each individual needs in his or her workstation, based on present use. The same documents will also indicate how each individual uses the materials they have, and what materials are used as part of the process each worker goes through as they perform the tasks assigned to them. Additional information will include any need for privacy, and the reasons. Survey documentation will indicate that additional amounts of space and additional furniture are necessary to accommodate whatever conference needs each individual employee may have.

The survey package will also provide the individual's in-person communication interface information, from which it will be necessary to produce an in-person communication matrix.

At this point all of the information must be either input into the individual's confidential computer database or entered onto a summary sheet. The first use of the information is to see if there are any areas in which the individual's stated needs exceed the accommodations of the basic workstation standard to which they are assigned. If there are areas that exceed these basic provisions, those areas are then examined to determine the legitimacy of the indicated needs.

Every contemplated change in a job description that will necessitate a change in storage or other work requirements for that job description should be factored in at this time. If the change is some time off, provision should be made at this time to ensure that the changes can be easily achieved at the actual time they become effective.

SHARED STORAGE AND EQUIPMENT

Most of the furniture, furnishings, and equipment will be accounted for by information contained in the individual workstation survey documents. While not a majority, a large amount in terms of quantity, and an even larger amount in terms of cost, the remainder of the furniture and equipment exists in places outside of the individual workstations. These items are normally the responsibility of one individual, supervisor, or manager even though their use is shared by more than one worker.

Of all the areas overlooked during planning of new spaces, shared equipment and furniture are the most likely to come under that category. Often this occurs because responsibility for these items is not clearly defined. Since such items are not located within anyone's individual workstation, no one feels that they are answerable for this furniture or equipment. Such items may at such a point *fall through the cracks* and not have space provided for it. If this fact goes unnoticed until after the move, programmed growth space will be used to accommodate it. Be certain that everyone and everything is provided for once and that nothing is provided for twice.

RELATIVE PROXIMITY

The relative proximity of the workstation of one individual to the workstation of another individual will obviously vary. The same is true about the relative proximity of one worker's workstation and a conference area where a meeting is being held, or the copy center where copies are to be made, or the men's room or women's room. Whatever the physical distance of each may be, it will cost the organization money.

Relative proximity is extremely important to three areas in the conduct of the business. These are

1. Workflow distances.
2. Travel distances to shared equipment and services.
3. Travel distances for face-to-face business conversations.

Individual for Workflow

Workflow, in the white-collar business world, is like the flow of blood in our bodies. Without an adequate blood flow the body dies. Without adequate workflow the business cannot thrive. Relative proximity, as it relates to work-flow efficiency, is an element of distance, which translates as an element of time, and which, in part, determines the cost and the efficiency of the process, each time the work flows from one processing workstation to another. Stating the obvious sometimes helps communicate a seemingly obvious, but for some mysterious reason, elusive fact. For that possibility alone I add that every effort is to be made to reduce the distance between processing workstations to the shortest distance possible. The reward will be well worth the time expended to accomplish the distance reduction.

Individual for Shared Equipment/Services

For the same reasons stated above, the same kind of proximity considerations must be applied to the use of remote, special equipment, and special areas that are shared. Each time workers leave their workstation to travel to a shared ser-vice area there is a cost involved. The relative proximity of each workstation to the location of the particular service involved is an element of the cost for each trip. This includes copiers, fax machines, and printers, as well as reproduction and supply areas. It is obvious that the workstation of every individual that uses the copier or the copy center cannot be located adjacent to either of those places. Consideration can be given, however, to the frequency with which each individual is required to use the various shared equipment or service. When weighed with all others with similar requirements, and when other factors are entered into the equation, *a best when all things are considered* location will be found. If such locations are found for each employee with such needs, the overall costs for the entire operation will be reduced appreciably.

Individual for Communication

Every time there is a necessary face-to-face business conversation between any two or more employees, there is a cost involved. The extent of that cost depends to some extent on how far each of the individuals involved has to travel to participate in the conversation. Although there is no universal answer to relative locations for every person who has meetings or who participates in conferences, some consideration for, and correlation between, the location patterns of those who will attend and the locations of those meetings and conferences will contribute to increased productivity. Letting the relative proximity of the majority of the participants take precedence over such things as the most prestigious location or rank of one of the participants when selecting the meeting location will help.

Relative Proximity Matrix

With all of your communication and workflow data assembled it is time to begin translating those data into useful tools by entering the information into one or more proximity matrices. Matrices such as these have historically been called *adjacency* matrices. You have no doubt noticed that whereas many individuals are placed adjacent to other individuals or equipment, intentionally, others are not. Although it appears that they should be, and your observation is correct, this situation occurs because at some point there was no space left immediately adjacent to an individual or service to place them. There is no way to arrange every individual immediately next to every other individual that communication patterns seem to indicate should be there. Everyone, however, will have a relative proximity, the location of which if properly identified and calculated will fit equally well in a number of locations. This gives you additional flexibility in your plan layout, while at the same time satisfying the functional needs of the planning process.

The same is true when you are considering the correct location for groups. Every group, like every individual, has a relative proximity as indicated by data that reported group interface as well as workflow. The flexibility allowed by the group's relative proximity indicator gives the planner much more latitude for placement with respect to any other single group or service entity. I recommend that you call your matrix a proximity matrix since it is a more accurate definition of what the matrix indicates.

POWER REQUIREMENTS

Many pieces of equipment from computer terminals and monitors to typewriters, calculators, pencil sharpeners, and radios require electric power for operation. Task lights also require power. Supplemental heaters in winter and fans in the summer need electric power. For the workplace to be planned to provide adequate electric power where it is needed, the data relating to that need must be provided to whoever is responsible for arranging for the work necessary to accomplish that end. Information in the form of specification sheets from the equipment manufacturer should be provided also. If such specification sheets cannot be obtained, then specific equipment information forms need to be completed for each piece of equipment for which there is no manufacturer specification sheet (see Appendix).

SIGNAL AND DATA REQUIREMENTS

Signal requirements relate to sounds or images that are transmitted, mostly over wire or cable of various types. Frequently when we refer to signal in the workplace it involves telephone equipment of some type. More specifically the reference is usually made to the installation and hook-up of telephone equipment such as power supplies, amplifiers, and switchgear, and telephone devices such as handsets, answering machines, and facimile transmitters, more commonly referred to as the *fax machine*. Wire conductors and cables used for transmitting voice, video, and data must be separated and run in conduit or cells other than those with wire carrying electric power, if unwanted sounds, noise, and other kinds of interference are to be avoided in the signals. Data requirements are similar except perhaps more sensitive. Cables carrying data are used to connect one device to another without splices or connectors in the actual cable.

All of the wire and/or cable that connect various elements of electrical and electronic devices, and the support equipment that accompanies them, must be placed somewhere, preferably out of sight but at the same time easily accessible. Some, but not all, systems furniture has electrical compartments, or raceways, as an integral part of the system panels. The size of these compartments varies as does the amount of wire or cable that can be accommodated in them. The cable and wire capacities of any systems furniture are very important now, and becomes more important with each passing year. Greater capacity usually translates to greater flexibility and greater ease of reconfiguration.

It is wise, in my opinion, to keep the wire in or on the floor for general distribution, bringing it up into the panel system or partitions when and where needed. Wire and cable distributed through the ceiling plenum is an inexpensive first cost way of getting power, phone, and data where you want it, then dropping power poles where you need to bring the services down. Unfortunately your workplace may soon look like a forest of telephone poles, and the ceiling, because of having ceiling board removed and replaced to accomplish the work, may soon begin to look unsightly.

The telephone company will normally have an equipment room, to their specifications, somewhere in your company's building. If it is a multistory building with a sizable floor area at each level, there will likely be a room on each floor where telephone panels and switches are located. If there are multiple tenants on the floor, the lines for your organization's phones will be run from the phone room on the floor to a phone panel in your own space. From that panel the wires are run to each individual phone, fax, or other device requiring phone service.

Planning, to establish your telephone and data equipment and cabling needs, should be of high priority for your projects. Lead times for some equipment are long and last minute delays can be prevented by knowing your requirements and placing your orders at the earliest date possible.

14

PLANNING THE SPACE

Several kinds of data, which have been collected and analyzed, will be utilized as you begin to plan the various areas of the workplace. These are related to

1. Workflow.
2. Face-to-Face Communications.
3. Electronic Communications.
    A. Face-to-Face Electronic Communications.
    B. Other Electronic Communications.
4. Written Communications.
5. Workstation Standards and Workmodules.

WORKFLOW

Workflow, as its name implies, is the orderly and organized movement of the paperwork of the business process as it moves from one individual to another until the process is completed. Each individual performs his or her task or tasks and passes the paper on to the next individual scheduled in the process. At the end of the process the paper is either saved or destroyed.

When the information contained on the paper or other material is saved, it will be stored, either in a file as is, recorded on microfilm and stored on a reel, or as microfiche on cards or unframed pieces of film and stored in trays or other containers. More and more information is being stored electronically, with no hard copies of any kind retained. There is the need to store electronic storage media, of course, but considerably more information can be stored in the same amount of space.

The storage options for electronic data are hard disk, floppy disks of various sizes and types, tape on reels, and compact laser disks. Each of these media is then normally stored in cabinets specifically configured for either a single media type or several different types according to the specific needs of the organization.

If the information is not to be retained, for whatever reason, the material will be thrown away. This process normally is as simple as placing the material in a trash container; from there the contents of the container are collected and removed to a landfill. If sensitive or confidential information is contained in the material being disposed of, then more attention must be paid to be certain that the material cannot have the information extracted even if someone is able to obtain access to the trash you are discarding. The most often used methods of rendering such material unusable are shredding it into very narrow strips or chaff, or in some cases incineration. The method selected is determined by the degree of sensitivity or confidentiality attached to the discarded information.

It is important, if maximum efficiency is to be achieved, that goals of orderliness and organization be priorities of the first order. Methods and procedures are elements of the Gamma Sector Controls and Limits and therefore are not dealt with here, except to emphasize their importance in the overall strategy to optimize the white-collar workplace.

Contributions to workflow efficiency that are derived from the Beta Sector are ease of movement of the process material to and through each work area, appropriate and ample storage space for pending material that must remain at any workstation while waiting information or other action, and minimum practical distance between individual workstation stops required in the process. The accommodation of information to be stored, the appropriate types of storage units or components for the material being stored, and, where necessary, the ability to lock the storage as well as the means to securely dispose of sensitive or otherwise confidential material are all within the index of Beta Sector options.

FACE-TO-FACE COMMUNICATIONS

Necessary face-to-face communication, meaning communication that is part of the business process and that is necessarily in person, as opposed to written or electronic communications, must be accommodated if workplace maximization is to be accomplished.

Simply stated in the extreme it means this. Suppose that the CEO of an organization must speak in person to the shipping dispatcher 40 times a day but must speak in person to the President of the company only twice each day. On the surface this information would indicate that either the CEO's office should be located on the loading dock or the dispatcher should have a space on executive row.

Relative proximity of one individual to others with whom frequent in-person business communication needs to occur must be determined based on total distance traveled by each person in order to accomplish the interchange of information. The well worn phrase *Time is money* is as true today as at any time past. Travel time for employees to move from their own place to the workstation of another is measureable and should be reduced to the least practical amount.

For the same reasons stated above, the same kind of proximity considerations must be applied to the use of remote, special equipment, and special areas shared by various individuals. This includes copiers, fax machines, and printers, as well as conference and supply areas.

ELECTRONIC COMMUNICATIONS

We have deliberately separated the requirements for face-to-face communications from those of written and electronic communications. The primary reason for this differentiation is the fact that in a majority of instances, it costs more to communicate face-to-face than by any other method. For electronic or written messages, it matters little if the intended recipient is ten feet away, four floors away in the same building, across town, or across an ocean from the sender. For face-to-face messages in any of the above situations the cost will be obviously more. Relative proximity within a single workspace, a single building, or even a complex of buildings is generally more controllable than between two or more sites. The same is true of more than a single site if the locations involved are separated by less than 15 minutes travel time by automobile or shuttle. This is a generalization and specific situations and conditions may indicate otherwise.

Face-to-Face Electronic Communications

Teleconferencing is the next best thing to being there. And although the availability of facilities may be limited and the cost is not necessarily inexpensive, it affords many of the advantages of face-to-face, in-person communications for a fraction of the cost, particularly when great distances and more than two people are included.

In large metropolitan areas teleconferencing facilities may be rented or leased from telecommunications providers such as the phone company or other service businesses. Where the need is sufficient various types of businesses install their own teleconferencing facility. If your organization has the need for such a facility and you intend to include it in the program you are planning, it should be included as part of the special purpose areas, sometimes referred to by architects and designers as ancillary areas.

Other Electronic Communications

Other commonly used electronic communication methods include telephone, facimile transmitters, radio, telegraph, telex, and cable. Each of these is a viable and efficient means of communications under certain circumstances. Each has advantages and disadvantages relating to time, cost, and security.

An important aspect that must not be overlooked regarding these devices, and the related electronic and mechanical equipment that is part of the total installation, is the space that must be provided for their placement, utilization, and maintenance. Specification sheets are provided by most equipment manufacturers for their equipment that will indicate the amount of clear space required surrounding each piece of equipment. If specification sheets are not furnished with the equipment, contact the manufacturer's representative for your area, or their customer service department.

WRITTEN COMMUNICATIONS

Written communications require only the provision of a surface on which to write and provision for storage of the materials that are used in the writing process. We are moving slowly into the age where electronic transmission and storage will be the overwhelming method of choice. It remains to be seen at what point a written signature gives way to another form of acceptable, and later preferred, concept of personal authentication of written communications and documents.

Year after year the opportunity to do things differently, and more efficiently, is presented and made available to businesses because a manufacturer has perfected the process or software that makes it possible and brought it to the marketplace. It is very often a long period of time, however, before this same capability is available in the majority of the world's workplaces, if ever. As I have previously indicated, substantial change most often comes slowly. Human signatures will be used throughout the lifetimes of most of those living in the year 2000 and beyond by most businesses and individuals. For quickly recording thoughts or notes, writing material and a writing instrument are still the most often sought, because of their simplicity, their convenience, and general availability. Watch someone in an airport with the smallest of electronic notebooks, or diaries, trying to note flight information. Many give up quickly and in desperation jot the information on a scrap of paper and move on. It will not always be that way, but that is the way it will be for quite a while into the twenty-first century.

Adequate light levels and quality are important for workers who must read handwritten material as part of their job. Veiling reflections caused by improperly designed lighting can make any reading material difficult to read. Handwritten material has the added problems of illegibility, size of the writing, and lack of contrast. These problems are distracting and they are loaded with fatigue factors. Be certain that the lighting in your workplace is of good design. There should be a consulting lighting designer for your projects. This most often will be a different person than the electrical engineer who will design the balance of the electrical portion of your project. A good lighting designer will cost you an additional fee. But like every other material, method, technique, and service that is proposed in this book, it is cost effective, and except in a very few situations you will see the return of all of the money spent on your project and much, much more.

WORKSTATION STANDARDS AND WORKMODULES

Standard workstations are covered thoroughly in Chapter 11. Workstation standards are allotments of space and are assigned based on the job description of each individual and the various tasks and responsibilities required therein. Total net space assigned to each individual is further determined by the workmodule attached to the job description he or she is assigned.

The same basic job title, because of variations in the task or equipment requirements from one job description to another, may have one of many workmodules or workmodule variations attached to it, requiring that different amounts of space be assigned thereto to accommodate the workmodule assignment.

One very important suggestion is that you maintain the integrity of your basic workstation standards. Do not create additional standards to solve special situations or unusual conditions. Such is the purpose of, and the time to use, workstation variations. Workstation variations are in existence to accommodate just such instances, and are to be returned to the standard as soon as the condition or the situation ceases to exist, however long that may happen to be.

There is a tendency, even a fondness, on the part of many designers to lay out office workspaces at some angle, other than perpendicular, to the perimeter walls, usually 45 degrees. This technique is used to provide more visual interest in the interior. Such visual interest, it is claimed, provides a less boring array of workstations, as opposed to row upon row of panels, all of the same height, with each either parallel or perpendicular to the rest.

Although it may be true that a plan that is rotated 45 degrees offers added visual interest, such a layout brings with it some facility management problems. The first problem is that the initial installation will probably be more expensive, if the work is done by an experienced installer, due to the additional time required to establish and maintain an angular grid with virtually no simple baselines, such as perimeter walls, to work to and to measure from. The same problem will reappear when any large segments of the workplace are to be reconfigured.

Another problem, perhaps the most important of all, is that any layout that is not 90 degrees with reference to the perimeter will require more area in which to place it. It is a simple geometric fact that when you enclose one square or rectangle inside of another square or rectangle the outermost shape must be larger if the inner shape is positioned any way but parallel (see Figure 14.1).

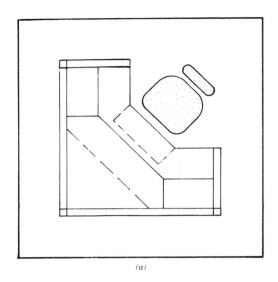

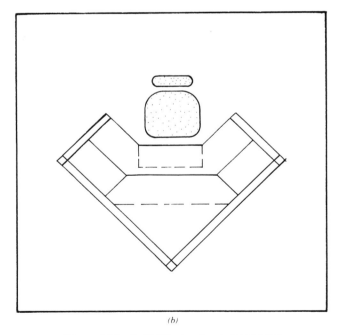

Figure 14.1. (A,B) Effects of angular layouts.

If the shape of the area is other than a square or a rectangle, the problem of layout is more complex. Circles or shapes with curved walls of any kind can be the most perplexing of all. These shapes can be used, but require special consideration if an efficient use of the available space is to be accomplished.

Experience has shown that when workplaces are originally planned in rectilinear spaces but with a layout placed at an acute angle, with respect to the perimeter walls, those workplaces when reconfigured are normally reworked into a linear or parallel plan (see Figure 14.2).

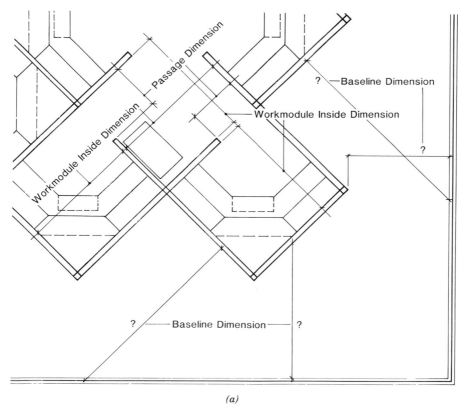

(a)

Figure 14.2. Space waste with angular workstation layout.

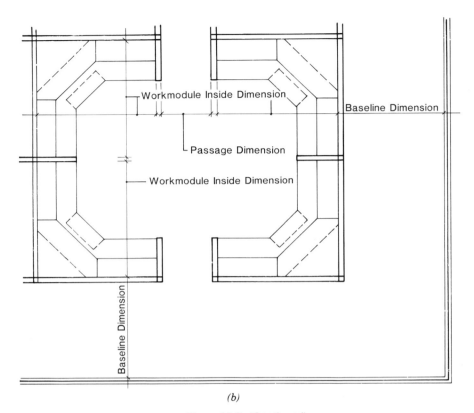

(b)

Figure 14.2. (*Continued*)

15

FACILITY MOVES AND MANAGEMENT

When the planning is finished, the design completed, and everything has been approved, the spaces that will contain the workplaces are soon to be finished and the furniture and furnishings are scheduled for delivery. What is left is the move from the old facility to the new. Logistically, the facility move involves many details that must be considered, adequately planned, and coordinated. The planning and coordination must apply to both internal and external aspects of the event. All the more so if the move is to be efficient, smooth, and with all costs, recorded or not, kept to a minimum.

THE FACILITY MOVE

The size of your organization will make a difference in the way certain parts of the move are planned and carried out. Every size organization, large, small, and in between, however, must deal with certain logistical specifics. The better planned, organized, and coordinated these are, the less disruptive and the less expensive the move will be.

Organizing the Move

A task that must first be accomplished is the appointment of a relocation director for the move. The director then appoints an assistant for each individual existing building involved in the relocation. If there is only a single building, but a number of floors, then an assistant for each floor may be appropriate and helpful. This group constitutes the Relocation Management Committee (RMC). The third task is to select members of the Relocation Coordinating Committee (RCC). The RCC is to be made up of representatives from each identifiable department or group. Each individual selected will act as the liaison and coordinator for his or her segment of your organization.

Each of these committees is temporary and will be disbanded following the critique that will be held after the move is completed and the organization is again functioning smoothly.

The Schedule

The next item to be accomplished is the preparation of the move schedule. The first schedule will be tentative and should be ready for presentation to and review by the RMC, and later the RCC, no less than 6 months before the actual expected move date. The schedule may be expanded or condensed to reflect the size and complexity of the organization. Essentially it will be similar to Table 15.1.

The first job of the RMC is to identify, insofar as possible, the realistic date on which the new workplace will be ready for occupancy. To determine when that date is likely to be will involve conversations with several different persons, depending on what work is to precede the occupancy of your workplace.

If your organization is constructing a new building then the contractor's representative is the person who should be able to tell you when your building will be ready to move into. If you are moving into a leased space that is being prepared by the realtor or developer from whom you are leasing, then information relating to when you can move in will normally be furnished by a representative from that company. If you are leasing space, but are responsible for your own improvements, then you will have to obtain information from each company, contractor, or anyone else who is involved in the preparation of your space or spaces.

TABLE 15.1. XYX Corporation Relocation Schedule

Date	Event
_____	Select relocation director
_____	Select balance of Relocation Management Committee
_____	Select members of Relocation Coordinating Committee
_____	Identify date new workplace location will be ready for occupancy
_____	Set primary relocation day
_____	Set contingency relocation day
_____	Be certain that furniture, furnishings, and equipment are on order; determine acknowledged ship dates for all of the above
_____	Select and interview at least three moving contractors
_____	Select moving contractor
_____	Prepare notification list
_____	Obtain change of address cards from post office

TABLE 15.1. (*Continued*)

Date	Event
————————————	Have announcement prepared
————————————	Contact the telephone company business office
————————————	Contact representative of the business and personal telephone directories in your area
————————————	Review printed matter situation; order only what you need to carry through to move
————————————	Revise printed matter as necessary or desired and order new supply to be delivered to new location immediately after move (the next day)
————————————	Review and revise insurance coverage
————————————	Conduct clean up, clean out operation
————————————	Have your architect or interior designer prepare relocation locator drawings
————————————	Prepare a relocation plan
————————————	Officially announce the move
————————————	Coordinate with your moving contractor
————————————	Schedule, and arrange to receive and distribute cartons
————————————	Investigate and schedule, if necessary, use of elevators at each end of move
————————————	Research labor union situation; make appropriate arrangements and if necessary change your schedule
————————————	Arrange for in-house orientation for telephone system and other specialized equipment
————————————	Arrange for and hold in-house open house
————————————	Plan for lost and found at each end of move; make everyone aware of their location and encourage their use by all
————————————	Arrange for sufficient trash receptacles; also arrange for them to be emptied during the move, as necessary
————————————	Coordinate and expedite the move
————————————	Hold general employee orientation
————————————	Expedite finding proper location for lost items
————————————	Thank everyone for helping make the move successfully; praise the committee members for their diligence and hard work; take them out to lunch or dinner (on the company, of course)

Furthermore, you will also have to contact vendors who will be doing preparatory work for various electronic devices that will be installed in your workplace, as well as others. These may include, but are certainly not limited to the telephone company, or companies, the computer service organization or whoever is running data cable for you, the security service, and the food service vendor. Your architect and your interior designer, if these are not the same individual or group, should be involved. The various vendors with whom you will work will need information about the space as well as access thereto. Having them coordinate through and with the architect will facilitate the entire move process. The ability of your company to operate efficiently from the time you move in is dependent on all of these firms having completed their work, including the hook-up of the equipment that will use these power, communication, and data cables. Some sensitive equipment must be moved only by companies who service them, not your mover, to protect the warrantee. Equipment that is sometimes in this category includes copiers and computers. Check to be certain.

We must not overlook the dealers who will furnish and install your furniture, systems furniture, and furnishings. These types of items, if ordered correctly and early enough, need not present a delay or other problems at the time of your move. It is one more place with which to coordinate before you set the date for your relocation. Ideally, at the time you are attempting to finalize the date for occupancy, and before you do finalize the actual scheduled move-in date, your furniture, systems furniture, furnishings, and equipment will be on order with an acknowledgment for a shipping date from the manufacturer in hand. The promised date will be a date you have requested based on your best information as to when occupancy can be accomplished and with sufficient time between the ship date and the occupancy date to allow for shipment, delivery, and installation.

After you are relatively certain that everything will be in order for relocation on the assigned date for move-in, set the contingency move date, or fall back position, in case the unimaginable occurs, goes wrong, happens, or whatever. A contingency date may be necessary because of an act of God, or because of an act of stupidity. It is not important to know which, because there are enough of each to more than go around, and either can be more than sufficient to unwind the best layed plan.

The Moving Contractor

Thoroughly investigate and interview at least three experienced movers to determine which will be able to do the best job for you and your organization. Best means more than having the lowest price. Best, in this case, means movers who will with care, courtesy, and sufficient kinds and quantities of the necessary equipment make your move quickly and efficiently, without damage, without unnecessary disruption, and without delays. Disruption and delay caused by inadequate equipment or insufficient quantities of items such as dollies, for example, can quickly make the promised savings disappear. Also having the equipment at the right building at the right time is important in keeping your move on time.

The mover will make available to you and help you estimate the number of cartons you will need. They will provide the very important information tags that identify each piece of equipment, carton, furniture, or whatever that is to be moved. The tag will show the exact place from which the item is being moved, as well as the exact place to which the item is being relocated. It is wise to have each person responsible for items include their last name on the item, also (see Figure 15.1).

Moving an organization requires a large amount of work and extra energy from every individual in the company. At the same time it is a wonderful opportunity for change and renewal; an opportunity to make operating and and standards changes that have been needed, but have been put off for various reasons. Such changes, when installed at the time of a facility move, can usually be accomplished with less difficulty and more cooperative acceptance by the majority of your employees.

Notification List

The RMC will cause a notification list to be prepared for use before, at the time of, and after the move. The list of those who should know about your move should include, but is certainly not limited to, the following:

1. Clients or customers
2. Banks and other financial organizations
3. Insurance agencies
4. All government agencies (federal, state, and city)
5. Vendors
6. Services
7. Newspapers
8. Magazines
9. Other subscriptions

Two items that must be mailed, and that the committee should be certain are properly prepared before mailing, are (1) change of address forms, which are available from any post office. Change of address cards are required, by the Post Office Department, to be sent to those from who you normally receive mail. These must be fully completed and mailed a sufficient amount of time before the move that delays or disruptions are eliminated, or at least minimized. (2) A nicely designed and printed mailer, formally announcing your move. The announcement can say whatever you please, but must include the following if it is to be of use to the recipient.

1. The name of your company.

2. Your company's new address (including street or box number, room or suite number in a building with more than a single tenant, city, state, and nine digit zip code, if possible, five digit otherwise).

3. All communication numbers that you care to include (phone, fax, telex, 800 numbers, cable, etc.).

4. The effective date of your move (When should the recipient start sending mail to your new address?).

5. A request that the recipient please change their records to reflect the new information.

Announcements in the form of a news release to the business editor of local newspapers is welcomed. In some instances you may even get a story about your business.

The Telephone Company

As soon as you know approximately when you will move and where, call the telephone company, or companies if you are dealing with more than one. Be certain that the phone company, or whatever company publishes the telephone directories in your area, white and yellow pages, knows of your pending move. In some instances phone numbers will have to be changed, lines added, and other changes made. The lead times for all directories are relatively long. If you do not want to go for a major part of the year with your phone not listed, start early with all divisions of the phone company that need to be aware of what you are going to do.

Printed Materials

Begin to deplete existing amounts of stationery and other printed items and order only sufficient quantities of the old materials to take you through the move. Begin also to plan for the replacement of all printed matter that has information about your present location and numbers. This is a great opportunity to redesign or otherwise change any formats, style, logo, or typeface of your printed materials. Again, lead times are relatively long, so planning, presentations, and decisions need to come early in the relocation process to prevent difficulties after the move.

Insurance

It is important to consult with your insurance representatives as well as your legal counsel about the matter of insurance. It is prudent at this time to review your coverage. Particular attention should be given to how the new location will affect your insurance coverage, and what, if any, changes will need to be made. Another item to be discussed will be your insurance coverage for all aspects of the actual relocation activities.

Clean Up and Clean Out

A pending relocation seems to make certain tasks less of a chore than would be the case at any other time. That includes the purging of files and the discarding of various items and materials that are of no further use to the organization. These items and materials have been retained for many different reasons, many of which have long since been forgotten. At any point in time most files can be purged by 30 percent with no effect other than the reclaimation of storage space in the files. Any item that has no immediate use, or no foreseeable future use, should be discarded.

Relocation Drawings

Two very important drawings are to be prepared for use before and during the move. These drawings are of every area, of every floor, of every building from which the organization is moving and to which the organization is moving. These drawings can be schematic, single line types of drawings. Those of the spaces from which the organization is moving indicate existing offices and workstations and as much furniture and equipment as possible. The drawing or drawings of the new workplace will indicate the new office, workstations, and all other places where furniture, furnishings, files, records, binders, supplies, and so on are to be placed. These drawings are primary tools that will be used by RMC, RCC, and the moving company. These drawings can be prepared by your architect, designer, or other consultant, usually as an extra service for an additional fee. If the drawings are correctly prepared, they will save more than the nominal fee that is usually charged for this service.

The occurrence of a facility move is a very good time to plan, not only for the move, but for the future as well. It is an appropriate time to retain a designer who is function oriented, but who also has the ability to provide visually pleasing workplaces, and develop with them a master plan for your workplace. A master plan will allow you to maximize the use of the space that you have and provide for anticipated future growth, and will include provisions for the flexibility to respond, easily, to the need for reconfiguration in the years ahead.

The Relocation Plan

The RMC is responsible for preparing the relocation plan. This plan is then documented in the form of a small manual, which will be distributed to each individual who has need of the information. After the manual has been prepared and the RCC has been selected, a meeting is held to indoctrinate the RCC members and explain the schedule, and their responsibilities regarding the total relocation plan. Once the schedule is established, it must be checked, verified, and updated regularly to be certain nothing has changed with the other parties involved—realtor, developer, contractor, vendors, dealers, suppliers, and others. It is also necessary to be certain that the in-house portions of the plan are unchanged and on schedule as well.

Announcing the Move

As soon as the schedule is known and the RCC indoctrinated, make a formal announcement to the entire organization. Do this preferably in a meeting or series of meetings with the entire workforce. The same kind of involvement by employees that I have spoken of throughout this book is just as important here. Any move of this type desperately needs every kind of cooperation possible. Involving your workers by keeping them informed is the right thing to do and will help to ensure their cooperation. It is important that each individual knows who his or her representative on the RCC is and that questions should be funneled through that person. Information from the RCC should also be distributed by that representative. In the selection of committee members it is wise to select personable, even diplomatic types of individuals, if at all possible. Everyone is not going to be happy with the move. Later information may be included in the newsletter if your company has one, or in memorandums.

Coordinate with the Moving Contractor

Have regular coordinating meetings with the moving company representative. Be certain that all in-house tasks are on schedule and that any additional information relative to the move is discussed with the representative to be certain that information has been transmitted to them and that it is being dealt with.

Cartons

Cartons will normally be supplied by the moving contractor as part of their contract. Be certain that there are enough cartons for everyone's use, and be certain that the cartons are distributed by the representative to those who will be packing them. This does not mean the committee representative has to personally deliver the cartons, only that arrangements are made so that everyone knows where to get them and when, and what to do with the cartons after they are received. Be certain individuals begin packing at the designated time for different types of records and materials and that everyone has their packing completed by the scheduled time for the move. It is very important that each carton is correctly marked according to instructions. Information on the carton must include the following:

1. The Area of Origination (Where the carton comes from).
2. The carton number (1 of whatever total of carton you have).
3. The total number of cartons you have.
4. The Area of Destination (Where the carton is to be delivered).
5. Your name (Name of person whose material is in the carton, or the name of the person who is responsible for the material in the carton).

The carton tag (Figure 15.1) will have spaces for several of the above items. These spaces must be filled out completely. If there is no designated space on the tag for part of the information, write the information on the carton with a large felt tip pen, and permanent, waterproof ink. Do not be shy! Print large enough so that it can be read. Be sure to securely attach the tag to the carton. Usually these tags have self-adhesive backs, so remove the paper liner material from the back and then press the tag firmly onto the carton. If your tags must be moistened, by all means supply plenty of sponge type moisteners and let everyone moisten away before firmly attaching the tag to the carton. In all too many instances tags are filled out but never attached to the carton. In other situations the tags are affixed to the wrong cartons. A little care by all involved can prevent a tremendous amount of lost time that will occur if individuals are not attentive when placing tags and other identifying marks and information on cartons with their own material, or cartons for which they are responsible. Actual label size should be 6 inches by 6 inches minimum.

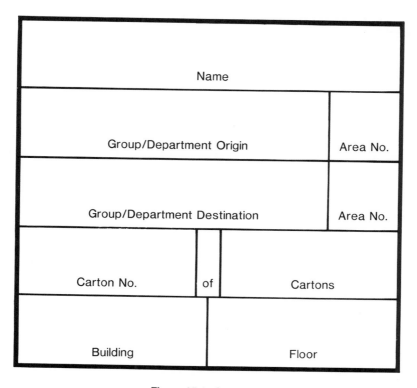

Figure 15.1. Carton tag.

In-House Open House

When the new workplace has been completed and is nearly ready for occupancy, an employee open house is a good way, in addition to indoctrinations described earlier, to introduce all employees to the new spaces. Including refreshments for all who attend is a nice, usually appreciated, touch. Again, including employees in the relocation process, in ways that do not involve work on their part, amounts to good employee relations, far out of proportion to the cost of such an event.

Telephone Orientation and Training

Frequently when moving to a new location, for various reasons the decision is made to purchase, lease, or otherwise obtain a new telephone system. At the earliest time possible after such a system is installed and is operational, employees should be instructed in its use. Such a seminar will normally be conducted by either the telephone system manufacturer or the dealer involved in its installation. The seminar may be at a training facility provided by the vendors involved or it may take place at the new location to which your firm is about to move. Wherever such training occurs is of less importance than the fact that it does occur and that it is thorough. It is important that employees are convinced that the features, when used, benefit not only the organization, but themselves as well. Most electronic phone systems are designed to be cost effective and to improve productivity. When the features that allow this efficiency are not used, no one benefits.

I was working in a consulting capacity with a corporate client and was trying to convince some of their executives of the value of making a necessary capital expenditure in order to accomplish an increase in their white-collar productivity. Every time I would mention the words *increased productivity*, I would be told, again, of complaints the company had about a new telephone system that was purchased based on a promise of *increased productivity*. Although admitting to some improvement, the complaint was that many of the features of the system were never used by the employees when there was a clear opportunity to do so. Two thoughts came immediately to mind, but I kept them to myself, however. The first thought I had as to why the system was not delivering as promised was perhaps that the system was not as good as it was claimed to be. Maybe what was being delivered was all the potential available. The second thought was that perhaps the workers were not adequately trained. Perhaps their proficiency was insufficient to deliver what the equipment was capable of delivering. Or, of course, it could the something altogether different.

Over the next several weeks I had the opportunity to spend time with a number of different workers at their desks while they were performing their various assigned tasks. It became obvious, quickly, that these individuals had been adequately trained in the use of the telephone system. It became equally obvious that when the use of a feature benefited the worker or made their own work easier, it was used regularly with proficiency. On the other hand if the benefit accrued only to the company, how well and how often it was used depended on how difficult the feature was to use. It is the same as in the case with the workstation chair. If there are more than two adjustment control devices on a workstation chair individuals react subconsciously to the complexity and do not use any of the controls. Ease of use is a very important consideration when selecting any equipment.

General Employee Orientation

A general orientation and information meeting with all employees is necessary, either prior to or immediately after the move. At the meeting information should be communicated relative to any changes in rules and regulations that have resulted from the relocation, such as but not limited to the following:

1. Security information.
2. Smoking limitations and areas (if allowed at all).
3. Work hours, lunch and break times (or flex-time limits).
4. Repeat information about lost and found areas.
5. Information relative to food and other services that are available in the surroundings of the new location.
6. Question and answer period. As in any such session, answer what you can. Obtain answers for questions you cannot immediately answer, and communicate the answer by memo the following day or just as soon as the answer can be obtained.

Elevators

For any company moving into a multistory building, unless you will occupy the entire building, elevator availability and scheduling are of extreme importance. In such a situation it is important to schedule your move on a day that does not have others in the building trying to do the same thing at the same time. Should that happen to you, you will find yourself sharing use of the freight elevator with others, greatly extending the time it takes for your move, not to mention the cost. The same can occur if your move is scheduled while your furniture, or that of others, is being delivered at the time of your move.

If other floors or parts of the building into which you are moving are still under construction, the freight elevators, or any elevator used to carry anything other than passengers, may have to be operated by a hoisting engineer according to the work rules for the project. The hoisting engineer is a union tradesman, furnished and paid by the general contractor, for the project and for construction related work only. Additionally, materials may not be moved onto floors above the first without the elevator being operated by the hoisting engineer. Arrangements for use of the elevators and the union operator must normally be made by the moving contractor, through the general contractor. The moving contractor will be charged for these services and those charges will be passed along to your organization. Be certain that this type of charge is included in your agreement with the moving contractor, if such a condition exists, but only if such condition exists.

Labor Unions

If the building into which you are moving is new, and parts of the building are still under construction, trade labor unions may take exception if your mover is not union. If you have new furniture arriving at the same time as the items that you are moving, including files, existing furniture, and so on, you may find your move halted while various trade unions sort out which work is going to be done by which union. For existing items you have movers that belong to the Teamsters Union and there are laborers that belong to the Building Trades Union. As long as all are union, the only complication to avoid is having the new and the old arriving at the same time. A properly executed schedule will not let this happen, regardless, because all new furniture, furnishings, and equipment should be completely installed before the move begins. In some areas work by trade unions is not required. It is a good idea to determine these facts, as applicable to your project, if you do not already have that information.

One more thought relative to the Building Trade Unions. If you are moving into a part of a building, whether it is a multistory low, or high-rise building, or a multitenant low building in a campus plan industrial park, the business of work being done by union trades may be an issue that you must deal with. For example, a project I was involved with was a start-up operation for an established manufacturer. Management made the decision to move the office into the new structure, even though the plant portion would not be ready for 60 days. Since the office staff was dealing with hiring and the purchasing of supplies, the move was appropriate.

A small part of the finish work in the office was still to be completed, however, after the move in. The painting contractor was known to have indicated, some time before they were selected, that their company was union, and for that reason were not asked again if they were still union. As it turned out, they were not. The firm was small and the bulk of the work they did did not require union workers. To reduce the firm's overhead the union membership had been dropped, a fact the company had not advertised. About 15 minutes after the contractor arrived on the jobsite, however, a union painter who was working in the plant portion of the project came to see the contractor to be certain that the new painting contractor on the job was also union. The new painter excused himself by saying he would not be on the job but those who were to do the work would be union.

The painter then proceeded to try to arrange with relatives, who were also painters but who were union members as well, to do the job for him. Because of prior commitments an arrangement could not be worked out. After a couple of days trying to work out a different deal, the painter finally said he would not be able to do the work. Another paint contractor was found, but at a greater cost and additional delays. All of this could have been avoided had a determination been made beforehand as to the painting contractor's current status with the union, on a project where a union contractor was all that would be allowed to do the job without having a picket line put up and the job shut down.

Move-Day Coordination

Finally the day arrives. Again depending on the size of your organization, there are certain things that you can do to ensure the greatest degree of success possible, given your particular circumstances. Communications are important. Keeping a phone line or several phone lines open between like points in each location can expedite the move and clarify questions instantly. For example, keep an open line between the accounting department at the old location and the accounting department at the new location during the time that material, furniture, and equipment involving that part of the organization is actually being moved. How many lines can be used this way is limited foremost by the number of outside lines you have at each location and how many departments you have that are in the move process simultaneously. Another way of accomplishing the same result is by renting good quality two-way handy-talkies, or cellular transportable telephones. Although some movers maintain communications between both ends of a move, some do not. It is important that dollies, pads, and other moving equipment not be allowed to accumulate at the new location, to the detriment of the old location where items are still being loaded. The ability to remind someone that all such items, which are available after being unloaded, be returned on the next returning van should not be ignored or overlooked.

Lost and Found

The first few days after the move is completed there will undoubtedly be some surprises discovered. Cartons, and in some instances even furniture, will appear in locations with absolutely no plausible explanation as to why they would be where they are. If everything is properly marked, however, it is a simple matter to direct the carton, or cartons, or furniture, to the place where each should be.

One of the features that is greatly needed is a lost and found area. Locate one at each end of the move and let everyone know what it is and where it is located. The instructions are simple: any item, except empty cartons, that cannot be identified as to origination point or destination is moved to the lost and found area. The RMC together with the RCC attempt to identify the item and get it to the person who has responsibility for it. Likewise anyone who is missing any item should contact the RCC representative and look through each of the lost and found areas.

Trash

Each designated group is responsible for breaking down and stacking all empty cartons, where directed by their RCC representative. Trash must not be allowed to accumulate, particularly because of the fire and other safety hazards that result. Adequate receptacles should be provided for use by individuals. Arrangement should be made to empty them as often as needed, so that the trash situation does not get out of control. Such effort will help to ensure that fire and safety problems do not occur.

MONITORING AND MANAGING THE WORKPLACE

There are two choices. You can control the space in the workplace or it can control you. What is described in this book is only the beginning. Any workplace because of the people, the individuals who work there, who spend a good portion of their waking hours there, is a living, dynamic thing. With your master plan, which is, remember, a framework within which to work, you will be able to monitor the functions that take place within the areas shown on the plan. When it is necessary to make a change, to increase the size of one or five groups and/or decrease the size of still another, by referring to the Master Plan and your Operational Plan, the moves are accomplished with the least amount of disruption to the entire organization.

It is important to maintain the integrity of your workstation standards. It is important to adjust those standards to accommodate unusual situations, always on a temporary basis. This process is part of the ability to control the workplace rather than having it control you and your organization, and keeping that situation from eventually preventing the continued high productivity yield brought about through your efforts with the Beta Sector elements.

Continued vigilance and effort is required to achieve all of the advantages and rewards that are inherent in the materials of the Beta Advantage Workplace. Take advantage of the features of your modular carpet. Rotate high wear areas to moderate or low wear locations and extend the life and improve the appearance of your workplace floor finish material. Be certain that your maintenance programs are adhered to, are operated properly, and are on schedule. Be certain that damage and stains are treated quickly and correctly. This is all part of monitoring and managing the workplace. Follow-up action is, of course, required also.

A Locator System

A facility manager once lamented to me that there was a time when relocating a white-collar worker meant simply picking up a desk, a chair, and a file cabinet, placing them on dollies, and moving them from one location to another. Now, he said, as he waved at the surrounding systems furniture installation, everything has to be disassembled, moved, and then reassembled, a lot of pieces to deal with. Another problem, the manager continued, is inventory. Just trying to keep track of where all of these parts are is a big job.

The problem of knowing where things are, whether the *thing* happens to be at the location of a light fixture that needs a new lamp, an electrical outlet that is on the floor beneath the carpet, or the location of the various components of your systems furniture inventory can be a formidable one at best, and at times can seem overwhelming.

A locator system can tame the beast, and can be installed with a little time and thought as the only real expenditures. Such a locator requires the superimposition of a simple cartesian grid over a plan of your workspace, your floor of a building, your building, or your complex of buildings (see Figure 15.2).

The ideal starting point is to obtain, if you do not already have it, a set of the architect's drawings for your building or building floor. These may be obtained from your real estate broker or the architect. If you are unable to acquire

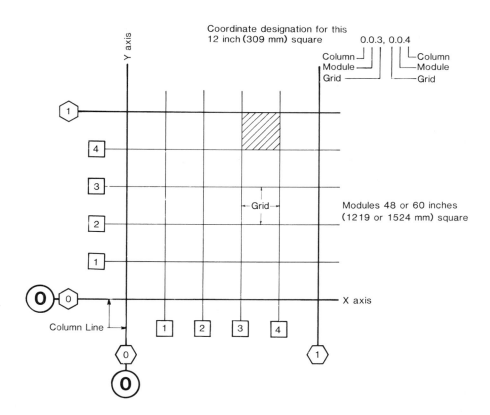

Figure 15.2.

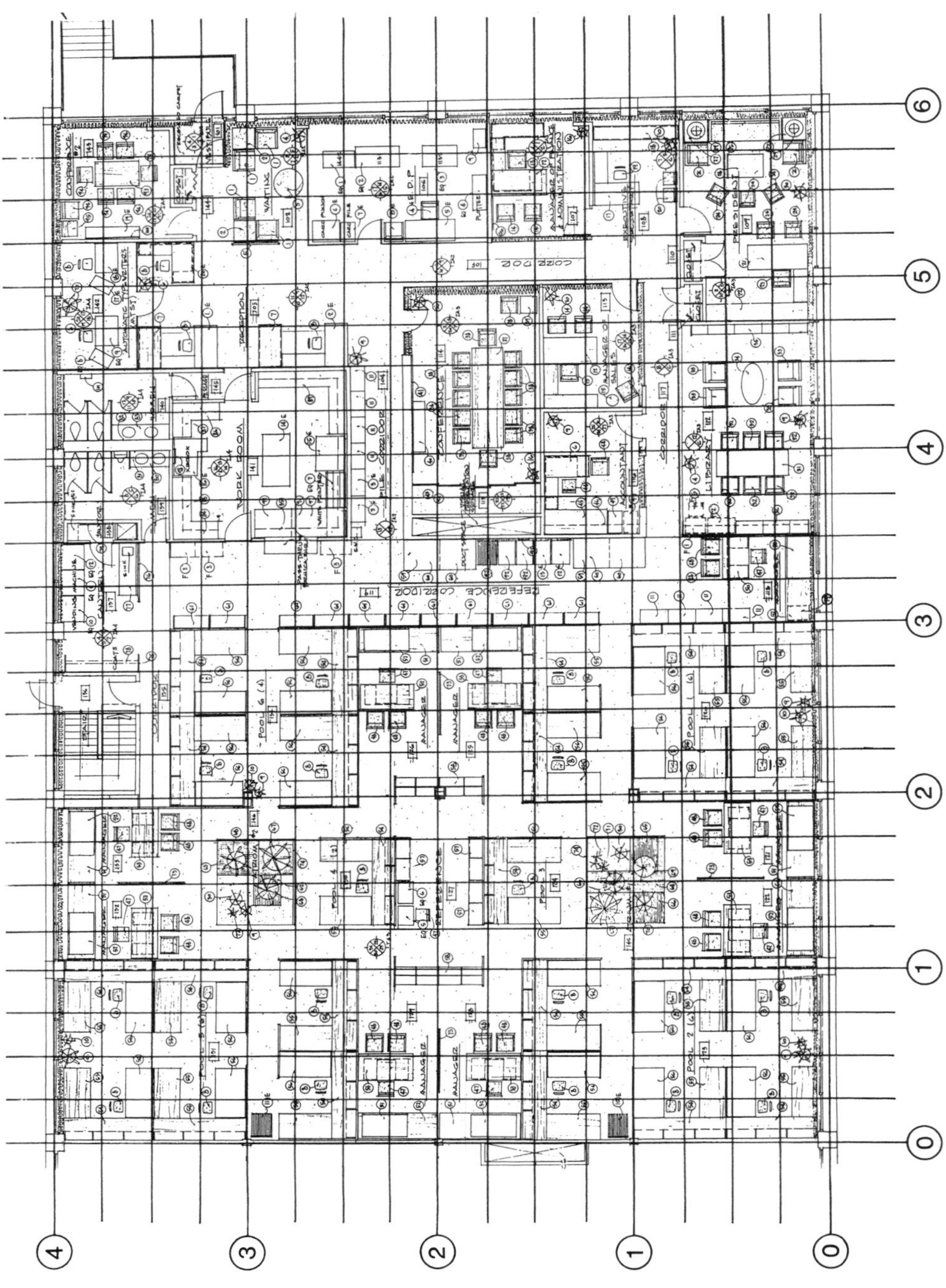

Figure 15.3.

the plans with either of these approaches, you can have a measured set drawn for you by your architect or designer. Whoever draws the plan, or plans, should measure and indicate on the drawing the center-to-center dimensions between all building columns, in each direction (see Figure 15.3).

Establish a grid of modules, preferably 48 inches (1219 mm) or 60 inches (1524 mm) center-to-center in each direction, on a piece of paper which is thin enough to see through. If neither of these grids will work to your column center lines, make your own grid that will. First trace on thin paper laid over the plan of your workplace the lines that run through the center of your columns in each direction. Divide the spaces between those lines into equal smaller spaces, as close as possible to 48 inches (1219 mm) or 60 inches (1524 mm) center-to-center in each direction. Next divide those squares into spaces that measure 12 inches (309 mm) center-to-center in each direction. Use a fixed cartesian coordinate system with the X axis indicating lines running left to right and the Y axis indicating lines running bottom to top of the drawing. The Z axis is a vertical axis and shows the number for the floor represented by the drawing beginning at the bottom for the lowest number. Number all lines. Begin with zero in the lower left corner of each drawing and number each horizontal line consecutively as you move up the page. Repeat the process to number the vertical lines, except your numbers will be consecutive, starting with zero, from left to right.

With the coordinate system you have just created, you or your employees, with minimal instruction, can locate specifically any 12 inch (309 mm) square in your workplace, and communicate that location to any other person who understands the locator system. Small subtle identification indicators affixed to interior columns and other landmarks will serve as guideposts to anyone as they proceed through the workplace seeking a particular location.

16

A LOOK INTO THE FUTURE

What is the future all about as far as white-collar productivity is concerned? The one certain thing about the workplaces of the future is that for some period of time they will not be all that different from what we have known until now. If we look far enough into the future, however, we will see something that by today's standards will at first appear radically different. On closer examination and consideration we will see that although the workstations and work-modules appear different visually, functionally they will be rather similar. Why? because except for workstations that will be fully automated and controlled by robots, the remainder will be restricted by the abilities and the limitations of humans, as they are now. Although productivity will have increased, as will be the speed and accuracy of the work, the basic ways in which information handling is accomplished will be very much as it is today.

An important thing to remember as we think about the future is that those conditions that limit what humans can do now, both psychologically and physiologically, are the conditions that will be limiting the workers of the future. Essentially those humans will be very similar to humans today.

Humans do not change the way they think or feel about various things very rapidly. Humans generally resist changing at all. Al Reis and Jack Trout, in their book *Bottom-Up Marketing*, speaking about the "Office of the Future," observe that

> In recent years, no myth has received as much hype. Yet the office of today looks a lot more like the office of the past than it does the "office of the future.*"

*From A. Reis and J. Trout, "Bottom-Up Marketing" (1989). Reproduced by permission from McGraw-Hill, Inc.

An advantage of the techniques and methods of Beta Sector productivity improvement is that there is no goal to change the way that individuals think, act, or feel. Such change can be accomplished only by the individuals themselves. Placing workers into the Beta Optimized Workplace will cause increased productivity on the part of most individuals.

As we have previously noted, humans change in physical size very slowly, having changed its longest dimension, height, only three inches in the past one hundred years. Further anthropologists generally agree that the human has stopped growing in stature, and barring some unexpected breakthrough involving nutrition that fact is not likely to change.

The need for flexibility and adjustability in workplace furniture and equipment is not to accommodate change in the size of any one individual, it is needed to accommodate the infinite number of different sized individuals who presently occupy the workplaces of today and the similar workers who will occupy the workplaces of the future.

Those who would improve the output produced by humans need to take into account what is already there and cultivate, promote, and support the tremendous potential that exists in each of us. Abilities must be recognized, multiplied, and amplified. Limitations must be recognized, minimized, and otherwise accommodated.

Not that long ago there was a great deal of conversation and writing about the "Electronic Office," the "Office of the Future," the "Electronic Office of the Future," or whatever name you would want to give it, and there was great concern with having the ability to accommodate the electronics that were soon to be found available for use therein. With few exceptions the only accommodations for the electronics being used in the workplace have been essentially relative to integrating, managing, and concealing wire and cable for power, signal, and data. As evidenced by problems that exist and will continue to exist for some time, those accommodations were extremely short-sighted and all too often inadequate.

I designed a "workstation for the future" in 1966 to support maximum efficiency and maximum productivity. That workstation, valid then, and just as valid now, will continue to be valid in the year 2025. It may look somewhat different by 2025, for one thing it will probably be a little smaller, but its basic functional concept will be the same.

The weakness of any workstation and its workmodules, whether then, now, or in the future, is and will continue to be the human individual that uses it. The worker is, at the same time, the weakest element, the strongest element, and the most expensive element of those parts that make up the workstation and its workmodule. That statement was true in 1966, is true now, and will continue to be true into the twenty-first century.

I felt quite certain that within 10 or 15 years of designing that superworkstation, every office would be equipped with, if not my design, something very similar to it. However, I assure you that every office does not have it, or anything like it. In my opinion, if one were to take a "today" individual and put them in that workstation, equip the workstation with "today" electronics, and have that person try to keep pace with the potential of the electronics therein, that individual could be largely destroyed, both physically and mentally in a time frame of 30 to 60 days. Why? because the bodies and minds of the workers of today are generally not acclimated, and as yet not suited, to the level of performance demanded by the capability inherent in much of the computers and their software that is available on the market today.

The human mind is capable of extraordinary things. And there is little question that even the surface of its potential has hardly been touched. Although there are always exceptions, the minds of a large number of our white-collar workers are not conditioned to receive information, analyze and evaluate it, add additional information from a number of sources, refer to still other information, compare the information to standards, calculate variances, process all of this information, make a decision, and formulate a response and enter it, all in the optimum, or less, time allowed for completing the task. And falling behind can be frustrating and intimidating. Each of these causes stress and unrelieved stress will destroy the strongest of us eventually.

Although humans are quite capable of developing the proefficiency required, it is going to take time. It will take the kind of time required for several generations of kids who challenge themselves with various sorts of high-speed electronic and computer controlled games to develop skill, accuracy, tolerance, and endurance.

Until these electronic speed wizards are available to us, and from that point on, since everyone does not as a child elect to participate in this type of electronic activity, workers will have to be conditioned, acclimatized, and slowly brought on line in the more efficient and productive workplaces of the future.

What will result is a corps of knowledge workers who will be able to perform, for periods of time, perhaps 60 to 75 minutes, of very intense, very accurate, and very productive work that requires continuous interfacing with various electronic information-processing devices. Some of these devices are now available and others will become available.

In this book until now we have not described the future. From the perspective of the productivity potential inherent in most white-collar workers, what we are proposing is very rudimentary. But it is something that every business can do now, and can get results now, and that is what we need, a place to begin.

What we are talking about in this chapter, however, is the future. It is where we are headed: workplaces where relatively short periods of individual effort will consist of periods of high intensity interchange with electronic devices. For some time into the future, perhaps forever, this type of activity will, I believe, have a tendency to overload the brain to the extent that there will exist the potential to destroy the brain, if there is no intercession.

How do you intercede? We have already seen that we are talking about a work period of 60 to 75 minutes. This, of course, is an estimate; the actual period may be longer or shorter. On completing the work period the individual proceeds to a neutralization and refreshment area that is located in close proximity to their workstation. There workers recline on a contour couch in an isolation unit where they select from thousands of audiovisual diversions. These presentations are intended to be soothing and relaxing with the goal of restoring the worker to a neutral level by compensating for the stress that was previously induced by the work period. Appropriate juices and other fluids are made available, offered, and encouraged, as well as an opportunity for some socialization perhaps, before returning for another period of productivity.

The physical movement during the productivity periods will be extremely limited. Presently such movement consists of minor finger, head, and eye movement. As voice input is further perfected, even the finger movement will no longer be necessary. Because of the existence of such conditions it will be essential to include at some point in the daily routine a period of physical activity, designed to maintain the physical health of the individual.

What we see is a cyclic kind of work format that combines intense productivity with periods of relaxation and physical activity during the course of a work day. The work day will be shorter, perhaps as little as 6 hours or even less. The productivity will be greater and the accuracy will be greatly improved.

The potential for increased productivity now is great. The potential for increased profit is likewise great. As we proceed on into the future the potential for further increases in productivity and profit will continue to grow by using the methods and techniques of the Beta Sector Solution to optimize the workplace.

These methods and techniques are real and will continue to increase productivity and increase profits as long as we do not lose sight of the most important fact relating to any attempts to improve productivity in general and white-collar productivity in particular. That is it all comes down to the individual. The individual cannot be ignored, the individual must be included, and the individual must be accommodated. To change the individual quickly is impossible except in isolated instances. To increase the individual's ability to produce and to help their organization make a profit is simple and certain as long as the above facts are accepted and the opportunity is provided.

APPENDIX

Table 1. Productivity Benefit Chart

Average annual salary		$18,000				Date:	
			Productivity Increase (%)				
Employees	10%	15%	20%	25%	30%	35%	40%
10	18	27	36	45	54	63	72
20	36	54	72	90	108	126	144
30	54	81	108	135	162	189	216
40	72	108	144	180	216	252	288
50	90	135	180	225	270	315	360
60	108	162	216	270	324	378	432
70	126	189	252	315	378	441	504
80	144	216	288	360	432	504	576
90	162	243	324	405	486	567	648
100	180	270	360	450	540	630	720
200	360	540	720	900	1,080	1,260	1,440
300	540	810	1,080	1,350	1,620	1,890	2,160
400	720	1,080	1,440	1,800	2,160	2,520	2,880
500	900	1,350	1,800	2,250	2,700	3,150	3,600
600	1,080	1,620	2,160	2,700	3,240	3,780	4,320
700	1,260	1,890	2,520	3,150	3,780	4,410	5,040
800	1,440	2,160	2,880	3,600	4,320	5,040	5,760
900	1,620	2,430	3,240	4,050	4,860	5,670	6,480
1000	1,800	2,700	3,600	4,500	5,400	6,300	7,200
2000	3,600	5,400	7,200	9,000	10,800	12,600	14,400
3000	5,400	8,100	10,800	13,500	16,200	18,900	21,600
4000	7,200	10,800	14,400	18,000	21,600	25,200	28,800
5000	9,000	13,500	18,000	22,500	27,000	31,500	36,000

Annual savings in thousands of dollars.

Table 2. Capital Expenditure Payback Chart

Date: 2 April 1990
Client: R. G. Robertson & Co.
Address: 4319 Humboldt Ave., Columbus, Ohio
Phone: (407) 374 6458
Contact: Mr. Ron Watson, Vice President

	Quantity Each	Cost per WS ($)	Area per WS (sq. ft.)	Total cost of WS ($)	Total area (sq. ft.)
WS 1	250	2,500.00	36.00	625,000.00	9,000
WS 2	125	3,000.00	48.00	375,000.00	6,000
WS 3	35	3,500.00	64.00	122,500.00	2,240
WS 4	12	4,000.00	100.00	48,000.00	1,200
WS 5	5	5,500.00	140.00	27,500.00	700
WS 6	2	6,000.00	256.00	12,000.00	512
WS 7	1	6,500.00	400.00	6,500.00	400
Totals	430			1,216,500.00	20,052

Total workstation area	20,052	sq. ft.
Total access area	6,016	sq. ft.
Total support area	3,008	sq. ft.
Total open plan area	29,075	sq. ft.
Total number of employees	430	
Total cost of environment—normal	$726,885.00	
Total cost of environment—premium	$981,294.75	
Beta advantage premium	$254,409.75	
Beta advantage premium factor	35%	
Total cost of workstations	$1,216,500.00	
Average cost per workstation	$2,829.07	
Professional fees	$50,130.00	
Total cost of project	$2,197,794.75	
Percentage of increase in productivity	30%	
Average annual salary	$18,000.00	
Annual savings	$2,322,000.00	
Square foot cost—normal	$25.00	sq. ft.
Square foot cost—premium	$33.75	sq. ft.
Payback period—workstations only	0.52 years	6.29 months
Payback period—environment only	0.42 years	5.07 months
Payback period—total	0.95 years	11.36 months

INDIVIDUAL WORKSTATION SURVEY

Date: _____

Introduction: As we begin to plan the interior of your new workplace, we need to learn as much as possible about the way you do your work and the area in which you do it. Your input is very valuable and necessary for the success of the project.

This survey is concerned only with what you have and use in your own personal workstation. If there is equipment located in your workstation that you share with other workers include that equipment on this form.

Any machines, equipment, files, or other kinds of storage that are located outside of your workstation and that are shared by others will be reported as part of a different questionnaire and should not be included on this form.

For our planning to be successful, we need to receive careful and thorough responses. Your full cooperation and participation will be appreciated.

Name: _____   Department: _____

Job Title: _____   Report to: _____

Length of time at present
job assignment: _____   Are you (LEFT) or (RIGHT) handed?
(CIRCLE ONE)

---

1. **Storage Information:** First we would like you to tell us about those materials that are normally stored in your workstation and how they are stored. We need to know the size of each material and the largest amount of each stored in the workstation at any one time.
    To help you identify the types of storage in your workstation and the method of measuring the quantity of material stored therein, please refer to the following examples:

A. Shelf Storage Information: The first information we need is about materials that are stored in shelves. Please indicate on the following chart such materials, their sizes, quantity (in linear inches), and the type of shelf storage used. Also indicate if storage units must be locked and how often the material is referenced or used in some way.

Material Description	Size L × W	Quantity (Linear Inches)	Shelf Type	Locked (Yes or No)	Frequency of Use[a]
Books					
Three-ring binders					
Catalogs					
Periodicals					
Forms					
Cards					
Computer printouts					
Boxes/bulk storage					
Supplies					
Files					
Coats					
Other					
Other					

[a]Frequency of use: 1, constant; 2, frequent; 3, occasional; 4, seldom.

Remarks:

B. **Drawer Storage Information:** Now we need to know about any materials in your workstation that are stored in drawers. Please indicate on the following chart such materials, their sizes, quantity (in linear inches), and the type of shelf storage used. Also indicate if storage units must be locked and how often the material is referenced or used in some way.

Material Description	Size L × W	Quantity (Linear Inches)	Shelf Type	Locked (Yes or No)	Frequency of Use[a]
Books					
Three-ring binders					
Catalogs					
Periodicals					
Forms					
Cards					
Computer printouts					
Boxes/bulk storage					
Supplies					
Files					
Other					
Other					
Other					

[a]Frequency of use: 1, constant; 2, frequent; 3, occasional; 4, seldom.

Please tell us if you have in your workstation more general office supplies such as paper clips, rubber bands, etc., than can be stored neatly in one small drawer? (Yes) (No) If your answer is yes, what quantity of such small office supplies do you have and how is it now stored?

Quantity: _____ How stored? _____

Remarks:

C. **Cabinet Storage Information:** The last bit of storage information we need concerns materials that are stored in your workstation that are stored in cabinets. Please indicate on the following chart such materials, their sizes, quantity (in linear inches), and the type of shelf storage used. Also indicate if storage units must be locked and how often the material is referenced or used in some way.

Material Description	Size L × W	Quantity (Linear Inches)	Shelf Type	Locked (Yes or No)	Frequency of Use[a]
Books					
Three-ring binders					
Catalogs					
Periodicals					
Forms					
Cards					
Computer printouts					
Boxes/bulk storage					
Supplies					
Files					
Other					
Other					
Other					

[a]Frequency of use: 1, constant; 2, frequent; 3, occasional; 4, seldom.

Remarks:

2. **Worksurface Information:** So much for workstation storage. Now we need information from you about those materials that you normally work with on your worksurface, while performing your job assignments.

A. While completing a job assignment, you will have on your worksurface a number of different work and reference materials **being used at the same time**.

Please circle, as illustrated in the sample below, each different combination of materials you use. Additional forms are available if you have additional combinations.

Example:

Files	Lists	Cards	Directory	3-Ring binder	Computer printout
Forms	Books	Checks	Periodical	Correspondence	Oversize drawings
Mail	Other: _____	_____	_____	_____	_____

Files	Lists	Cards	Directory	3-Ring binder	Computer printout
Forms	Books	Checks	Periodical	Correspondence	Oversize drawings
Mail	Other: _____	_____	_____	_____	_____

Files	Lists	Cards	Directory	3-Ring binder	Computer printout
Forms	Books	Checks	Periodical	Correspondence	Oversize drawings
Mail	Other: _____	_____	_____	_____	_____

Files	Lists	Cards	Directory	3-Ring binder	Computer printout
Forms	Books	Checks	Periodical	Correspondence	Oversize drawings
Mail	Other: _____	_____	_____	_____	_____

Listed below are miscellaneous items that might normally be found on a worksurface.

Please circle those items that are normally kept on your worksurface.

Calendar pad	Tape dispenser	Memo box	Rolodex	_____
Pencil cup	Telephone index	Stapler	_____	_____
Ash tray	Pencil sharpener	In/out tray	_____	_____

Remarks:

B. **Reference Material Information:** Please tell us about materials you refer to while performing your job assignment. We need to know the size of those materials and how often each is used during the day.

Material Description	Size L × W	Constantly	Referred to Frequently	Occasionally	Normally Kept
Lists					
Directories					
Records					
Files					
Forms					
Correspondence					
Binders					
Cards					
Large papers					
Mail					
Other					

Please indicate on the chart above where each reference material is normally kept when not being used?

1. Shelf over worksurface.   2. Desk drawer.   3. Tack surface.
4. File drawer.   5. _____   6. _____   7. _____

Remarks:

C. **Machine Information:** We now need to determine if there are machines or pieces of equipment that you work with **on your worksurface** while performing your job assignments and how much of the time each is used during the course of a day.

Description of Machine	Size (L × W)	No. Hours Used/Day						Shared? (Yes or No)	With Whom
		0-1	1-2	2-4	4-6	6-8	8+		
Typewriter manual/electric									
Memory typewriter									
VDT/CRT/PC									
Microfilm viewer									
Microfiche reader									
Dictator									
Transcriber									
Calculator									
Adding machine									
Printer									
Telephone									
Other									
Other									

Do you use, in your workstation, any other machines or equipment that are not on your worksurface? (Yes) (No) (CIRCLE ONE)

Equipment	Size (L × W × H)	Hours Used/Day

If your answer to the last question was yes, is the equipment shared with anyone? (Yes) (No) If yes, whom? _____

Remarks:

3. **Work flow Information:** Now please tell us the size and largest quantity of materials that come into and go out of your workstation each day. Please tell us also if the material can be put into a single group, or must be divided into separate groups.

Material Description	Size (L × W)	Quantity of Materials (Linear Inches/Group)					
		Group 1	Qty	Group 2	Qty	Group 3	Qty
Incoming Material: material that comes to you for your job function							
Pending material: material that must be held by you until completed							
Outgoing material: finished material that is ready to be passed on							

Remarks:

4. **Person-to-person Communication Information:** Finally tell us if you have meetings or conferences in your workstation. (Yes) (No) (CIRCLE ONE)

If the answer is yes, please indicate below the number of meetings held each week, the number of people in attendance at the meetings, and the approximate length of time required for the meeting.

Number of Persons Attending Meeting	Number of Meetings per Week						
	Less than 15 min	15 min– ½ hr	½ hr– 1 hr	1–2 hr	2–3 hr	3–4 hr	4 hr+
1							
2							
3							
4							
Other							
Other							
Other							
Other							

Remarks:

We would like you to tell us now any thoughts or ideas that you may have that you feel would improve your own workstation and make it easier for you to perform your work.

Thank you very much for your help. We will use your information, along with that of your fellow employees, as we plan and design your new offices. We expect that you will find the new facility an enjoyable place to be and, more important perhaps, a place that will help make your work easier and more pleasant to perform.

Yours truly,

M. Glynn Shumake, AIA

SHARED EQUIPMENT SURVEY

Date: _____

Introduction: In addition to the information we need about individuals and their workstations, we also need to know about those items that are not assigned to an individual, and are shared by more than one person in your organization.

This questionnaire asks for information about materials, equipment, furniture, storage units or facilities, and special work or conference areas used or shared by the employees and management of the organization.

Again, your careful and thorough responses will help to ensure successful planning of your facilities. We appreciate your continued cooperation and participation.

Group/Department Name: _____ Supervisor: _____

Report to: _____ Information by: _____

1. **Storage Information:** First we would like to know about materials that are normally stored for use by the employees of your group or department and how they are stored. We need to know the largest size of each material and the largest amount of each stored at any one time.
   To help you identify the types of storage and the method of measuring the quantity of material stored, please refer to the following examples:

A. **Shelf Storage Information:** The first information we need is about materials that are stored in shelves. Please indicate on the following chart such materials, their sizes, quantity (in linear inches), and the type of shelf storage used. Also indicate if storage units must be locked and how often the material is referenced or used in some way.

Material Description	Size L × W	Quantity (Linear Inches)	Shelf Type	Locked (Yes or No)	Frequency of Use[a]
Books					
Three-ring binders					
Catalogs					
Periodicals					
Forms					
Cards					
Computer					
Boxes/bulk storage					
Supplies					
Files					
Other ( )					
Other ( )					
Other ( )					

[a]Frequency of use: 1, constant; 2, frequent; 3, occasional; 4, seldom.

Remarks:

B. **Drawer Storage Information:** (NOTE! All file cabinets are to be listed later in the survey). Now we need to know about any materials that are stored in drawers. Please indicate on the following chart such materials, their sizes, quantity (in linear inches), and the type of shelf storage used. Also indicate if storage units must be locked and how often the material is referenced or used in some way.

Material Description	Size L × W	Quantity (Linear Inches)	Shelf Type	Locked (Yes or No)	Frequency of Use[a]
Books					
Three-ring binders					
Catalogs					
Periodicals					
Forms					
Cards					
Computer					
Boxes/bulk storage					
Supplies					
Other ( )					
Other ( )					
Other ( )					

[a]Frequency of use: 1, constant; 2, frequent; 3, occasional; 4, seldom.

Remarks:

C. **Cabinet Storage Information:** Now we need to know about materials that are stored in cabinets. Please indicate on the following chart such materials, their sizes, quantity (in linear inches), and the type of shelf storage used. Also indicate if storage units must be locked and how often the material is referenced or used in some way.

Material Description	Size L × W	Quantity (Linear Inches)	Shelf Type	Locked (Yes or No)	Frequency of Use[a]
Books					
Three-ring binders					
Catalogs					
Periodicals					
Forms					
Cards					
Computer					
Boxes/bulk storage					
Supplies					
Other ( )					
Other ( )					
Other ( )					

[a]Frequency of use: 1, constant; 2, frequent; 3, occasional; 4, seldom.

Remarks:

D. **File Cabinet Storage Information:** Now we need to know about materials stored in freestanding panel-mounted file cabinets. Please indicate on the following chart such materials, their sizes, quantity (in linear inches), and the type of shelf storage used. Also indicate if storage units must be locked and how often the material is referenced or used in some way.

Material Description	Size L × W	Quantity (Linear Inches)	Shelf Type	Locked (Yes or No)	Frequency of Use[a]
File folders, letter, top tab					
File folders, letter, end tab					
File folders, legal, top tab					
File folders, legal, end tab					
File folders, letter, hanging					
File folders, legal, hanging					
Books					
Three-ring binders					
Catalogs					
Periodicals					
Forms					
Cards					
Computer printouts					
Boxes/bulk storage					
Supplies					
Other ( )					
Other ( )					
Other ( )					

[a]Frequency of use: 1, constant; 2, frequent; 3, occasional; 4, seldom.

Remarks:

E. **Special Storage Information:** Tell us about any materials you have that require a special type of storage. Please indicate on the following chart such materials, their sizes, quantity (in linear inches), and the type of storage needed. Also indicate if storage units must be locked, any special secure storage required (see below), and how often the material is referenced or used in some way.

Material Description	Size L × W	Quantity (Linear Inches)	Shelf Type	Locked (Yes or No)	Frequency of Use[a]
Books					
Three-ring binders					
File folders (letter)					
(legal) (top tab)					
(end tab)					
(hanging)					
[circle all					
that apply]					
Computer tapes					
Computer disks					
Cash					
Punched cards					
Checks					
Invoices					
Requisitions					
Other ( )					
Other ( )					
Other ( )					

Special security types: A, safe; B, vault; C, fire protected file.
[a]Frequency of use: 1, constant; 2, frequent; 3, occasional; 4, seldom.

Remarks:

F. **Change in Storage Requirements:** We need to know if any of the storage requirements you have listed have undergone any kind of change during the past year? Please indicate on the chart below any such change.

Storage Type	Increase (Lin. In.)	Decrease (Lin. In.)	Is Change Expected to Continue?		
			Yes	No	Don't Know
Open Shelf					
Closed Shelf					
Drawer					
Cabinet					
File					
Special					
Other ( )					
Other ( )					
Other ( )					

Remarks:

G. **Machine Information:** We now need to determine what machines or pieces of equipment that are used by your group or department primarily, as well as specifics about such equipment.

Description of Machine	Size L × W	Manufacturer	Model No.	Frequency of Use[a]	By Whom
Typewriter Manual/Electric					
Memory Typewriter					
VDT/CRT					
Microfilm Viewer					
Microfiche reader					
Dictator					
Transcriber					
Calculator/Adding Machine					
Printer					
Telephone					
Other ( )					
Other ( )					
Other ( )					

[a]Frequency of use: 1, constant; 2, frequent; 3, occasional; 4, seldom.

Note! Please furnish a specification sheet for each piece of equipment listed. The specification sheet or sheets prepared by the equipment manufacturer are preferred. If such specifications are not available and cannot be obtained, please complete a Specific Information Form, including as much of the requested information as possible and attach to this survey.

Remarks:

H. **Special Use and Work Areas:** Please indicate what special use and work areas you now have or need to have in the new facility. Indicate on the following chart what areas are to be furnished.

Are Designation	Approximate Size	Special Requirements
Vestibule		
Reception area		
Library		
Computer room		
Cafeteria		
Mail room		
Printing Area		
Supply room		
Closed circuit TV center		
Security		
Other ( )		
Other ( )		
Other ( )		

Remarks:

I. **Conference Areas:** We need to determine facts about your conferences and meetings. Please indicate below the number of meetings held each week, that will not be held in anyone's individual workstation, the number of people in attendance at the meetings, and the approximate length of time required for the meeting.

Number of Persons Attending Meeting	Length of Meetings						
	Less than 15 min	15 min– ½ hr	½ hr– 1 hr	1–2 hrs	2–3 hrs	3–4 hrs	4 hrs+
Indicate number of meetings per week							
1–4							
5–7							
8–10							
10–12							
13–15							
16–20							
20–24							

Other

Remarks:

We would like you to tell us any thoughts or ideas that you may have that you feel would improve the workplace. Information concerning detrimental conditions that exist, and ideas you may have that you believe would make it easier for you and your workers to perform your work.

Thank you very much for your help. We will use your information, along with that of your fellow employees, as we plan and design your new offices. We expect that you will find the new facility an enjoyable place to be and a place that will help make your work easier and more pleasant to perform.

Yours truly,

M. Glynn Shumake, AIA

SPECIFIC EQUIPMENT INFORMATION

Date: _____

Please furnish specific information about any existing equipment or machine that is to be relocated to the new facility. Furnish also specific information about any new equipment or machines which will be purchased for use in the new facility.

Group/Department: _____ Information by: _____

Name of Equipment: _____ Manufacturer: _____

Present exact location:

Exact new location:

Attach manufacturer's specification sheets (all). If specification sheets are not available and cannot be obtained, please furnish as much of the information listed below as applies to the specific equipment described above.

Dimensions:

	Width	*Depth*	*Height*
Inches	_____	_____	_____
Millimeters	_____	_____	_____

Service clearances:

	Front	*Rear*	*Right*	*Left*
Inches	_____	_____	_____	_____
Millimeters	_____	_____	_____	_____

Weight: _____ pounds _____ kilograms
Heat output: _____ btu/hr _____ watts
Airflow/min: _____ ft/min _____ 1/s

Power requirements:
Voltage   _____   Phase   _____
Amps   _____   Watts   _____
Power cord _____   Plug type _____

Operating environment:
Temperature
Relative humidity
Maximum wet bulb

Nonoperating environment:
Temperature
Relative humidity
Maximum wet bulb

Ventilation required because of:
Noxious odors   _____
Heat   _____
Contamination   _____

Water service:
Volume _____ temperature _____ pressure _____
Connection _____ type _____ size _____

Drain:
Liquid to be drained _____
Connection _____ type _____ size _____

GLOSSARY

Ancillary Area: An ancillary area is a specific allotment and assignment of space for use in the performance of specialized functions, and which is normally for the use of any qualified individual or group that has a need for its use.

Ancillary Area Workmodule: An ancillary area workmodule is the specific allotment and assignment of furniture, furnishings, and equipment based on the functional requirements and the status level of the area.

Fatigue Factors: Fatigue factors are relative values that indicate the difference between the extent of the human fuel expenditure for one necessary condition, when compared to the fuel expenditure for a different substitute condition, because of and specific to any item or combination of items that we use or come into contact with. There are no exceptions and there are no neutrals; each item and its specific conditions will have a fatigue factor. It may be great, small, or any position between.

Sensory Distraction: Sensory distraction is conscious or unconscious disruption of a task-related thought process caused by extraneous sights, sounds, smells, or other stimuli. Such distraction may be inadvertent or intentional.

Special Purpose Area: A special purpose area is a specific allotment and assignment of space for use in the performance of specialized functions, and which is normally for the use of the specific group to which it is alloted and assigned.

Special Purpose Workmodule: A special purpose workmodule is the specific allotment and assignment of furniture, furnishings, and equipment based on the functional requirements and the status level of the area.

White-Collar Productivity: White-collar productivity is the result that is produced by workers performing the tasks that are required by the job description assigned to each individual worker.

White-Collar Productivity Potential: White-collar productivity potential, as relates to the Beta Sector, is the result that can reasonably be expected to be produced by workers performing the tasks that are required by the job decription assigned to each individual worker, under a specific set of interior environmental conditions and workstation/workmodule specifications.

White-Collar Workplace: The white-collar workplace is the area in which white-collar workers perform the various tasks that are part of their work. It is the total inside physical space or spaces that is occupied by information processors and that is divided into smaller spaces called workstations. Workstations are assigned to individual workers according to the tasks of their job description and their functional relationships with other workers and/or groups of workers. The workplace also includes special purpose areas and ancillary areas.

Workmodule: A workmodule is the specific allotment and assignment of furniture, accessories, equipment, and other appointments based on the functional needs of the individual worker, as indicated by that worker's job description and the status assignment of their position or title.

Workstation: A workstation is the specific allotment and assignment of space in the workplace where a specific task or series of tasks that are described in an individual worker's job description is to be performed by that individual worker or group of workers. This allotment of space is, or should be, based on a combination of functional need and status assignment exclusively.

SUGGESTED READING

*Dreyfus, Henry, *The Measure of Man: Human Factors in Design.* New York: Whitney Library of Design, 1967.

*Flynn, John E., Arthur W. Segil, and Gary R. Steffy, *Architectural Interior Systems*, 2nd ed. New York: Van Nostrand Reinhold, 1988; First edition, 1970.

Harris, David A., Alvin E. Palmer, Susan H. Lewis, Ralph Gerdes, David L. Munson, and Gershon Meckler, *Planning and Designing the Office Environment*, 2nd ed. New York: Van Nostrand Reinhold, 1991; First edition, 1981.

Kelley, Robert E., *The Gold Collar Worker.* Reading, MA: Addison-Wesley, 1985.

Makower, Joel, *Office Hazards.* Washington, DC: Tilden Press, 1981; paperback, out-of-print.

Mandel, A.C., *The Seated Man*, 2nd ed. Denmark: Dafnia, 1985; first edition, 1974; second edition, 1983.

*Panero, Julius, and Martin Zelnick, *Human Dimension and Interior Space.* New York: Whitney Library of Design, 1979.

Wineman, Jean D., editor, *Behavioral Issues in Office Design.* New York: Van Nostrand Reinhold, 1986.

*Design criteria and information included.

INDEX